SOMETHING'S TROUBLING ME

SOMETHING'S TROUBLING ME

How To Calm And Shape Difficult Professional Conversations

ANDY BETTS

with illustrations by Philippe Tur

ICONDA Publishing

Copyright © 2024 by Andrew Keith Betts, ICONDA Solutions

All rights reserved. No part of this book may be reproduced in any manner whatsoever without written permission except in the case of brief quotations embodied in critical articles and reviews.

First Printing, 2024

This title is also available in French:
QUELQUE CHOSE ME DÉRANGE
Apaiser et Façonner vos Conversations Difficiles Professionnelles

*"It is not because things are difficult that we do not dare;
it is because we do not dare that they are difficult."*
Seneca

*To Federica, Luke, Malika, Olivier, and Ulrika,
with heartfelt thanks for your support, patience, and daring.*

FOREWORD

If you struggle with difficult conversations and have not yet found reliable techniques for dealing with them, this book is for you. While difficult conversations are too subtle and complex to allow a simple "one size fits all" solution, they can be described in simple terms and images. Starting from such a description, I present an approach that will allow you to tackle difficult conversations effectively and confidently.

Such conversations are extremely varied, and as a professional coach, I am constantly amazed by surprising new examples.

For instance, a client–I'll call him Gerry[1]–came to one of my coaching sessions saying, "Something's troubling me." He complained of feeling awkward attending inter-company meetings with his boss. The latter, according to Gerry, was "out of touch" and gave a feeble impression of himself. As a result, attendees from other companies would assume that Gerry, and not his boss, was leading their organization. This situation was very uncomfortable for Gerry, and he struggled to express the emotions troubling him so much.

Uncomfortable emotions often disturb professional life. However, uncertain about how to deal with them, the people involved often avoid the issue which is causing the discomfort.

I am pleased to say that, equipped with the techniques I will describe, Gerry found the confidence and courage to talk openly with his manager about their relationship, and their candid exchange resolved the issue.

It is essential to deal quickly with awkward situations such as this one, even if you'd prefer to put them off. Procrastination lets problems accumulate and grow, damaging relationships. Therefore, recognizing and tackling them promptly is a life-enhancing skill. It positively impacts the world.

Maybe you picked up this book with your own conversational experiences or current challenges in mind. Do any of the following scenarios apply to you or remind you of others?

- Confronting unacceptable behavior, such as offensiveness, insensitivity, or obstructiveness.
- Dealing with poor performance, failure to achieve targets, unmet commitments, or broken promises.
- Giving bad news or talking about a personal problem: a negative report, a missed promotion, hygiene, or loudness, for example.
- Saying "no" to a request from a superior, a customer, a partner, or an enthusiastic colleague.
- Responding to frustration while conversing with a superior, a customer, a partner, or a colleague.
- Making a big "ask," e.g., for money, promotion, or forgiveness.

In the following pages, I'll describe my Candid and Calming Communication methodology and illustrate its use with my experiences and those of my close acquaintances. Though the cases I consider mainly stem from the professional world, you'll find them relevant in other areas of life as well.

What's more, you will find in the annex a pictorial summary of the methodology—a brief overview of everything—and a versatile set of exercises called Lights, Camera, Action! This unique resource will allow you to play around with difficult conversations safely, on your own, and with others.

Andy Betts
Crolles, May 2024

CONTENTS

Introduction	1
Don't Panic	3
Candid and Calming Communication	13
Pause	27
Ask	49
Listen	68
Explain	85
Staggered Conversations	110
Goodbye to the Troll	121
Epilogue	132
ANNEX	**133**
Pictorial Summary	134
Methodology Fundamentals	147
Lights, Camera, Action!	160
Notes and References	210
About The Author	221

Introduction

Difficult conversations are daunting. Intense emotions cloud your thinking and disrupt your ability to reason. Everyone involved is similarly affected, leading to tense, awkward interactions that only worsen matters.

Therefore, before addressing any divisive issues, you all need to feel more comfortable so that you can be more effective.

But, for the moment, it's as though there's a troll in the room, embodying all the negative feelings in the encounter. As long as he's around, you can't work anything out.

Your priority, then, is to persuade the troll to leave.

To do this, you have to shape the conversation, managing emotions on both sides of the table, starting with your own. At the same time, you look out for any conversational mischief, checking that the other party is as keen to find a Win-Win solution as you are. If not..., well, we'll discuss that later in the book.

Don't Panic

A troll is trouble. He is the highly charged, emotional aspect of a difficult conversation, fueled by conflicting viewpoints and interests[2]. He's a serious health and safety hazard!

When emotions are running high, they can cause panic. They can throw things off course and make it hard for the parties concerned to think clearly. Though emotions shouldn't be suppressed (it is only thanks to them that you know when something is wrong), they can be distracting and aggravating.

When trolls are about, people tend to become aggressive, fearful, or confused, and it becomes tempting to avoid awkward, inconvenient, but important problems.

However, avoiding an emotionally charged issue is like trying to sneak past the troll and escape. You do this because you can't stand the discomfort of a necessary conversation, but when the troll realizes what you're up to, he's more upset than he would have been if you'd confronted him in the first place!

At other times, you're just impatient to reach your original objective of, for example, getting information, agreeing on something, or reprimanding someone. You storm ahead, ignoring the troll in your hurry to achieve but lose twice over—you neither resolve the emotional issue nor reach your objective!

To understand how to avoid panic and the trap of emotional reasoning, let's examine a few of the major factors that attract trolls.

The group context

Conversations can involve:

1. Only two individuals
2. Two individuals in a group setting
3. An individual and a group.

While professional communications often occur in groups, most of them involve one-to-one interactions *within* a group (the second case in the list above). The presence of observers amplifies stress, so this case is particularly interesting. The troll is very likely to appear in such circumstances.

The group context also introduces a significant additional difficulty: the workplace focus on solutions, actions, and productivity. When something goes wrong in the communication between two people in a group, those unconcerned by the problem may become impatient to get on with the main business of the meeting. They don't want to "waste time" while two people sort out their differences. These additional aspects—lack of time and the scrutiny of onlookers—further exacerbate the situation.

To make matters even worse, the people involved in the exchange may have hidden needs. Perhaps the difficulty they face is rooted in an earlier traumatic event that one of them has experienced, or maybe there is an underlying trust issue unrelated to the problem at hand. Remember, however, that the workplace isn't the best place for healing psychological wounds or providing deep emotional support—and a workplace group setting is probably the worst place for it! You thus need to adjust your ambitions and expectations accordingly and think about what you can achieve in such a context.

Finally, you may also interact with a group, speaking to an audience but not to any particular individual. This situation is beyond the scope of the present text. Although I'll touch on live public conversations and social media discussions (synchronous and asynchronous communication cases), my focus is on the individual interactions within those contexts.

The impact of remoteness and delay

Distance often forces us to use text or recordings to communicate with others. This results in staggered, or "asynchronous", conversations, where one person does not get an immediate response from another. Such conversations are quite different from synchronous ones, where the parties involved are either physically together or connected by telephone or video conference, for example.

Until recently, asynchronous conversations were almost entirely undertaken by the exchange of letters and restricted to one-to-one or one-to-a-few types of communication.

It may seem hard to believe now, but people used to write letters to friends with the idea that they would be handed around, allowing everyone to catch up with their news—after a considerable delay, of course. Today, a simple CC instantly does the trick.

However, the impact of email, as impressive as it seemed at first, now seems trivial compared to internet-based forums and social media platforms. Just as email (and, later, chat) displaced paper-based conversations, forums and social media have created new types of conversations. Until they appeared on the scene, communication with more than a few tens of people was a unidirectional affair, achieved mainly through magazines, newspapers, and television. Now, anyone with a smartphone can debate with thousands of others.

Email, chat, forums, and social media have created new possibilities for difficult conversations, and it is natural to ask if there are best practices associated with these communication channels. Before addressing this question, let's first identify the most important distinguishing characteristics of these channels.

- Anyone can publish.
- Messages, posts, and other publications may reach unknown recipients.
- Responses may be received from anonymous senders (including machines).
- Responses may be publicly visible.
- Deliveries are almost instantaneous.

I suggest that the effect of these new communication possibilities is much more significant than, say, the impact of replacing in-person meetings with video calls and webinars. Sure, you had to learn some new tricks when adopting Zoom and Teams ("I can't turn my camera on!", "You are on mute," "Sorry, my battery is low," etc.) However, you were still dealing with the same human connections. In contrast, recent advances in asynchronous communication have changed the level of connectivity, so the disruption is far more significant.

I've used one-to-one conversations (in individual or group contexts) for most of the examples in this book. They illustrate the best practices that also apply to asynchronous contexts, with surprisingly few differences. However, a couple of these differences are significant:

- The quality of your written messages must be much higher than your spoken ones.
- You mustn't make assumptions about when, where, or how written communication will be received.

Despite these differences between synchronous and asynchronous conversations, you'll see later that the fundamentals don't change, only how they are applied.

Assessment tyranny

Assessment tyranny[3] is a constant hazard when attempting to resolve a difficult conversation. I refer to it frequently when I describe the Candid and Calming Communication methodology.

When you observe, you take sensed data (what you see, hear, read, etc.) and make *interpretations, evaluations,* and *predictions.* The combined effect of this interpretation-evaluation-prediction process is an *assessment.*

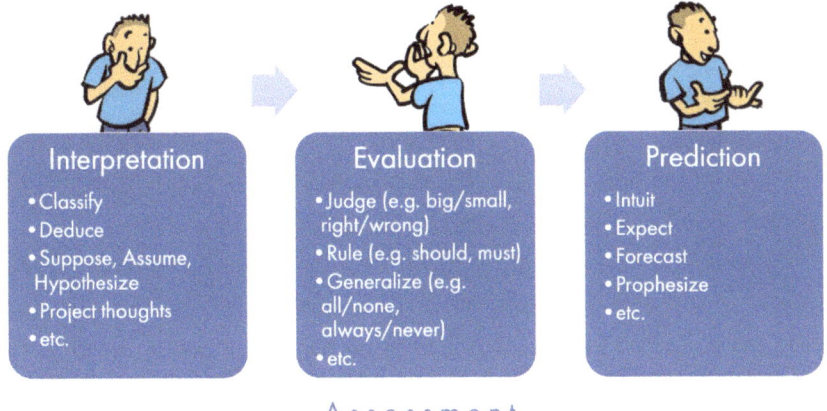

For example, suppose that you are a designer in a medium-sized company. There is a production line, and you just heard that the staff has gone on strike. Lacking any details about this event, you could explain the news in many ways, including the following:

- "I suppose the production staff want more money (interpretation). In my opinion, they're crazy to strike (evaluation), as it will jeopardize jobs by speeding up automation (prediction)."

This is fine. On the other hand, tyranny would occur if you presented your assessment as obvious and unquestionable—as if it were so evident that no reasonable person could deny it. Based on the example, you could make the following tyrannical assessment:

- "It's because the production staff wants more money. They're crazy! They'll get themselves replaced by robots."

In this second version, you state your interpretation, evaluation, and predictions as if they are indisputable facts instead of acknowledging that they are subjective. Your assessment can provoke a negative reaction when presented this way, especially if the atmosphere is tense.

Of course, assumptions, judgments, rules, etc., are necessary and useful, and you don't always have to go to the trouble of highlighting their subjective nature. For example, when you're relaxing at the Spaghetti House with friends, it's quite acceptable to say, "This pizza is awesome! Those guys in the kitchen are on a high tonight. They'll get a Michelin star if they keep this up!"

It would sound odd if, instead, you proclaimed, "*In my opinion*, this is an awesome pizza. *I think* the kitchen staff must be particularly enthusiastic this evening. If they continue producing food of this quality, *I believe* they could be in the running for some sort of industry recognition."

Brevity is fine when there are no trolls about, but when there is tension, it's advisable to speak carefully and qualify what you say to avoid misunderstanding.

In the context of a difficult discussion, assessment tyranny presents two principal dangers:

- When you use it in spoken conversation and writing, it may trigger an adverse reaction.
- When you use it in your internal dialogue (your self-talk), you may mistake your interpretations, evaluations, and predictions for facts.

Returning to the production strike example, when you say, "It's because the production staff wants more money. They're crazy! ...," you're assuming knowledge of what production workers are thinking and judging their actions. This could provoke a strong emotional reaction if the person you're addressing doesn't agree with you.

Contrast the above statement with, "I suppose the production staff wants more money. In my opinion, they're crazy to strike." By conceding that your assessment of the production staff's thinking is based on an assumption and that the evaluation of their action is just your opinion, you give the other party room to respond constructively. Disagreeing with your statement but less emotionally triggered than when facing a projection and a judgment, they might reply, "I disagree ..." This would put the conversation on an intellectual plane instead of an emotional one.

The above examples show that an assessment becomes tyrannical due to the subtle interactions between you and another person. Sometimes, both of you recognize interpretations, evaluations, and predictions without labeling them. On other occasions, particularly when there is a troll in the room, it is best to highlight them when you speak and write.

Getting into this habit would be straightforward if you were aware of all the assessments you make. Unfortunately, this is not the case, and your self-talk is polluted with tyrannical assessments, which leak into what you say out loud. For example, if you get into the habit of saying to yourself, "Our stupid management has done X" instead of "Our management has done X, which I disagree with," then you risk permanently associating "stupid" with your management. Consequently, this label can slip into your speech at the most inconvenient moments.

Once you forget that your assessments are subjective, they quickly become tyrannical. They pollute your internal dialogue, making your thinking less accurate. The story you tell yourself about whatever situation you are in becomes distorted, and your judgment is impaired.

The unexpected

As discussed, the group context, remoteness, and assessment tyranny often catalyze or exacerbate difficult conversations. However, they are certainly not the only causes.

For example, one of my professional roles is software sales, and when I wrote to a particular customer recently about their annual license renewal—a banal email—their CEO sent me an unexpected response. They complained stridently about annual price increases, which they considered unfair.

Their message contained aggressive language and focused on long-standing, perceived injustices. They also referred to recent business difficulties but did not say what they were. Attempting to reply to the hostile email without being defensive, I responded only with a question about the business difficulties. I also expressed my surprise since I had the impression that they were busy and successful.

Unfortunately, my reply triggered a furious response, and the business consequences were considerable.

Having absorbed the CEO's fury, I worked with my colleagues to understand what to do next and what had triggered such anger. My partner suggested that my observation of their business could be interpreted as a criticism. I wondered if my decision to reply with a question, rather than responding to the criticism of our pricing or perhaps apologizing for it, had been poorly received. My colleagues had other ideas, but none of them were correct, and when we did discover the real source of the CEO's discontent, we realized that it could not have been anticipated.

This exchange demonstrates how difficult it can be to predict another person's response to your words, however well-prepared they may be. Things that you consider positive may be construed quite differently by someone working in a different context than yours. Their triggers are not the same as yours, and when you don't know what they are—and, perhaps, when you assume that they will be thinking along the same lines as you are—it is easy to set off an emotional explosion inadvertently.

The bottom line is that the troll can turn up unexpectedly in any circumstances. There is, therefore, no way to craft a working environment or a living space that will permanently keep him out. Even by living alone in a remote cave, you cannot escape him—as we'll discover later in this book, he's quite able to break into your internal dialogue, your self-talk.

Hence, you must know how to deal with him effectively, and to do this, I suggest the Candid and Calming Communication methodology.

Candid and Calming Communication

Candid and Calming Communication (CCC) comprises the following:

- A hypothesis: achieving calm is a prerequisite to progress
- A mindset: a state of mind favoring an appropriate reaction at the onset of a difficult conversation
- A method: what you can do when you see a troll

Calm is a prerequisite to progress

CCC emphasizes what we should concentrate on at the start of a difficult conversation: achieving calm. Not a gritted teeth, stiff-upper-lip kind of calm, with emotions boiling beneath the surface, nor the robotic type of calm achieved by eliminating emotions. Instead, a genuine calm, with emotions present but not overwhelming the proceedings. You hold them just within earshot: audible but not drowning out your reason.

Great leaders are known for their ability to stay calm and transmit that calm to others. Think about how Nelson Mandela handled South Africa's transition out of apartheid, for example. Imagine what would have happened if he'd come out of prison and, once in power, called upon his downtrodden brothers and sisters to rise up and crush the white oppressor!

This example illustrates the importance of re-establishing a calm dialogue and demonstrates the colossal effort required to achieve this apparently modest goal. Remember that achieving calm is just an intermediate objective. Mandela's legacy is that he gave his country a chance to solve its social problems—not that he came up with a miracle cure for all its woes.

Unfortunately, historical counterexamples that contrast Mandela's approach are easy to find[4]. When leadership is lacking or leaders deliberately inflame emotions, people die in droves.

An anti-panic mindset

It's easy to panic when you realize that a difficult situation requires some particular action and that you must initiate it.

At the pivotal moment in a difficult conversation, hesitation, uncertainty, confusion, and self-doubt can creep over you.

Unfortunately, no methodology or technique will eliminate this feeling of panic. Time seems to be frozen. When you face a troll, it's less a question of *doing* something and more of *being* the type of person who doesn't panic.

A strong and appropriate mindset is needed. It will give you a solid foundation for using the techniques described in this book and fill you with confidence to ward off panicky reactions. The mindset you carry around makes the difference between staying in control and responding with an uncontrolled fight, flight, or freeze reaction.

A mindset is a default attitude, like an app permanently running in the background, automatically switching in at the right moment, and reacting appropriately to unexpected, emotional, panic-inducing events.

A mindset is also unique. No two people have precisely the same attitude toward their fellow human beings, of course, and I don't intend to describe an ideal mindset. I would like to suggest, however, that it would include the following:

- Positive initial assumptions (pre-suppositions)
- A systemic attitude (with a "nudge & adjust" approach)
- A combination of honesty and benevolence

Let's look at these ingredients.

Positive initial assumptions

The following are the pre-suppositions[5] I wish to suggest:

- People function perfectly (they are okay and don't need to be fixed).
- People make the best choices for themselves in their perceived circumstances.
- Every behavior has a positive intention.
- Every behavior is useful in a certain context.

Note that these are *initial assumptions* for any professional conversation. One may apply them to other areas of life, but I advise against making them into a dogma and using them regardless of the circumstances. When I go out cycling, for example, I make dramatically different pre-suppositions: it's safer to assume that everyone else on the road is incompetent, so I cycle more carefully!

Moreover, note that you should verify a pre-supposition since it is only an assumption[6]. These precautions notwithstanding, you're in a much better position to resolve a difficult conversation if you begin with this frame of mind.

A crucial benefit of these pre-suppositions is that they help you avoid the mistaken assumption that others see things as you do. They force you to consider the other person's point of view. You can no longer just write off their displeasing behavior as incompetence or dishonesty—instead, you must look carefully at other possibilities.

A systemic attitude (with "nudge and adjust")

After starting with optimistic pre-suppositions, I suggest that having a systemic attitude to what follows is much more effective than an analytical one.

An analytical approach to problem-solving is typically used for complicated, artificial systems, such as cars and computers. You first focus on finding the fault—the *source* of a problem—supposing that when you fix that fault, the whole system will work again. This approach works well when replacing a faulty spark plug or repairing a buggy line of code, for example.

On the other hand, a systemic attitude is more appropriate when you are interacting with people and organizations[7]. These are so complex that we rarely understand an issue's root cause. The problem belongs to the system and cannot be attributed to just one of its components. Furthermore, these components may change spontaneously—people get sick, groups reconfigure, organizations have turnover, and so on—and the effects of such changes are unpredictable.

A fundamental principle of systemic theory is that systems are better understood by focusing on the relationships between their elements than by considering each in isolation. When you take this point of view, you see things differently compared to what you'd see with an analytical approach.

However, although systemic thinking can help you better understand a situation, you cannot improve that situation by talking to the system. You must interact with a person or a group of people, bearing in mind their relationships to other system components, including yourself. If this sounds tricky, that's because it is.

Hence, when faced with a difficult conversation, instead of attempting to fully understand why the situation is not as you would wish to be (the analytical approach), you use nudge and adjust tactics. With a systemic attitude, you accept that whatever you do may not work out the first time. Therefore, focusing on your present intentions, you do your best to say something helpful and assess the other party's response. This is the first nudge. You then adjust your ideas and make further nudges, gradually influencing things in the intended direction.

This discussion is beginning to encroach on the topic of leadership. As discussed, a systemic approach involves trial and error, which implies proactivity. When using this approach, depending on what happens in the conversation, you take the initiative and consciously decide your next move. Even if you choose to say nothing or to withdraw, you are deciding something. A degree of leadership is thus unavoidable.

By leadership, I don't mean it in the sense of you being the official and organizationally appointed leader in the room—instead, I refer to the spontaneous leadership involved in making decisions based on a situation's demands.

For example, you must take a leadership stance when you encounter people who have not dedicated time to building their difficult conversation skills. They will quickly recognize your confidence in handling the situation, showing the same relief as when a doctor or nurse takes charge of an emergency. People know competence when they see it and are happy to let experts take the lead.

In difficult conversations, sometimes you have to take the lead, even if you don't have as many stars on your uniform as those around you.

Honesty and benevolence combined

Most people would agree that honesty and benevolence are both virtues, but many sense a conflict between them in a difficult conversation. On the one hand, it seems important to disclose information and criticism honestly, but on the other, you want to be kind. Appropriately combining these two imperatives is key to effectiveness (Levine).

However, too much honesty will kill you, just as sure as none at all (to echo Freddy Mercury's words).

When benevolence is lacking, *brutal* honesty tends to result—you might reveal a piece of information without being mindful of the hurt it may cause another person. For example, you may tell someone that they are disliked or are considered incompetent, though there might be perfectly effective ways to move the conversation forward without saying this. Brutal honesty may cause a person on the receiving end to react with the fight, flight or freeze response: they could violently resist, withdraw, or stay rooted to the spot, not knowing what to say next.

At the same time, if you practice insufficient honesty, you avoid discussing important topics because you fear the discomfort caused by uncomfortable truths. And if you show benevolence but do not act honestly, you are probably offering false hope or encouragement.

Note that accurately expressing oneself is *not sufficient* to achieve honesty. For example, you can inform a colleague that they have been put forward for a job—an accurate statement—without mentioning that someone else is sure to get the position. The colleague was put forward only to satisfy bureaucratic requirements. You would be dishonest and guilty of lying by omission if you failed to mention this essential piece of information.

Finally, the absence of both honesty and benevolence implies uncaring manipulation.

Kim Scott[8], an American author, draws attention to these points, suggesting that the most effective attitude to adopt in communication is a combination of caring personally and challenging directly—she calls this intersection *radical candor* (Scott).

Of course, life tends to produce situations in which finding the right balance of honesty and benevolence is challenging, and everybody must decide where the tipping point is for themselves.

Self-reinforcing

Each difficult conversation that you successfully resolve will strengthen your mindset and increase your confidence regarding the effectiveness of your positive initial assumptions, nudge and adjust tactics, and your ability to take the lead. It will become easier for you to dive into the next encounter without panic. This way, you establish a virtuous circle of practice reinforcing theory and theory driving improved practice.

The candid exchange

To bring calm to a difficult conversation, it is necessary to have a candid exchange.

On the surface, a candid exchange is no different from a regular productive dialogue. You ask questions, listen, explain your point of view, and occasionally pause for thought. However, although a candid exchange also has these four components, it requires special care, discipline, and the skilled use of the techniques described in this book. Therefore, a candid exchange differs markedly from a familiar workplace conversation, as we shall see.

The possible outcomes of a candid exchange might be the following:

- Settlement: calm is achieved, the troll leaves the room, and we move on to dialogue.
- Controlled failure: recognizing danger, you consciously choose between a fight, flight, or freeze response.
- Uncontrolled failure: despite your best efforts, the conversation degenerates into psychological games (Berne), or the relationship breaks down.

I believe that a candid exchange is so important that I've made it the focus of this book. I'll concentrate on the period from when the troll enters the room until he leaves it.

Once you return to dialogue, the remaining work may require negotiation and pitching skills or some job-specific capability. However, I believe these are best learned independently. Furthermore, as I've already mentioned, they have no place in a candid exchange.

Of course, I'm not devaluing these skills. I've written about negotiation and other communication tools in past publications (Betts), and there exists a lot of great material on these topics[9]. Moreover, you may already possess finely tuned negotiation skills. Supposing you have, I am confident that once you have mastered candid exchanges, you will have no trouble combining them with negotiation in the larger framework of a difficult conversation.

> ### *False friends*
> *People whose first language is French may find my use of the words "candid" and "frank" difficult to understand, as they are false friends of the French words* candide *and* franc. *"Candid" is*

best translated as franc, *whereas the meaning of the French word* candide *is approximately "naïve."*

Phases of a difficult conversation

Ideally, a complete conversation will look like this:

| RITUALS, PASTIMES, DIALOGUE | ⟷ | CANDID EXCHANGE | ⟷ | DIALOGUE | ⟷ | FINAL RITUALS |

People spend their time in six different ways: withdrawal, rituals, pastimes, dialogue, games, and intimacy[10].

In the diagram, the beginning of the conversation might be something like the following:

"How's things?"
"Could be worse. And you?"
"Fine, thanks!"
"Did you see the match last night?"
"Yeah, ... blah, blah."

These are *rituals* and *pastimes*. From here, the proceedings evolve into professional *dialogue*—discussions of work-related matters—either because the individuals don't want to address a lurking difficulty or because they haven't yet noticed it. A dialogue is a rational discussion, perhaps not wholly free of uncomfortable emotions but not dominated by them.

Assuming that a meeting is not disturbed by *withdrawal* (for example, people don't turn up, leave early, or stay and remain silent), it tends to follow the following sequence: rituals → pastimes → dialogue. However, when difficulties arise, dialogue ceases, and the conversation can go in two directions: games or intimacy.

Games, mentioned briefly above, are unproductive, repetitive sequences where both sides receive short-term but negative payoffs, such as self-justification, a sense of victory, or confirmation of victimhood. However, whatever the short-term gain, the core issue is not resolved[11].

On the other hand, *intimacy* occurs when people talk sincerely and honestly to each other and discuss their viewpoints, feelings, and needs. It results in better mutual understanding and a closer relationship, even if it is not necessarily one of friendship. In this sense, in a candid exchange, you're in intimate contact with the other party.

Whether you foresee a problem and expect a troll in the room or if he is an unwelcome surprise, a candid exchange is the only way to sort things out.

If all goes well, this exchange allows you to better appreciate each other's viewpoints and interests, thereby calming emotions and allowing you to return to calm dialogue. This dialogue should follow naturally from the candid exchange—but in a different spirit. You can now deal with complex and touchy subjects rationally and ideate and negotiate more effectively and comfortably.

A course alteration

How should you proceed after deciding to deal with the troll? The first thing is to step aside from operational matters. You must alter course.

> *Put operational matters completely aside until calm is achieved.*

It's vital to deal with the emotional content of a difficult conversation before attempting to reach an agreement, discuss plans, or do any of the other myriad things we do at work. These action-oriented tasks will only become possible once the troll leaves the room and emotions no longer overwhelm the proceedings.

> *Have a candid exchange with the sole objective of achieving calm.*

Therefore, you should focus on the troll and have a candid conversation with the other party to achieve calm.

Note that the conversation is not over when you are done with the candid exchange. Having achieved this, you are back to productive dialogue and can discuss the next steps, action plans, and so on. Hence, a difficult conversation and a candid exchange are different things, and a difficult conversation may contain one or more candid exchanges.

> *The truly difficult part of a conversation ends once negative emotions cease to dominate it. Then, and only then, with the troll out of the room, can you return to operational matters.*

But what if you fail to return to dialogue? If the troll refuses to leave the room, a *controlled* fight, flight, or freeze may be necessary.

Controlled fight, flight, and freeze

A controlled fight is your best option when, during the candid exchange, you become convinced that the other party is determined to obtain a Win-Lose outcome—and especially if there is a threat to you or the people you care about. In this case, you take a defensive stance, which could mean, for example, escalating the issue to management, taking legal action, or even initiating a physical struggle.

In the same situation, a controlled flight might be the only option when the other party is much more powerful than you. Perhaps it is impossible to get help from management because the other party's political influence is too strong. Realizing this, you could decide to withdraw. In a commercial situation, you might accept a deal you consider unfair but represents the least bad outcome. Alternatively, you could take a moral stand and refuse an offer which, although materially better than nothing, you despise.

A controlled freeze allows you to return to the conversation another day. If you find that a candid exchange is stuck—both parties seem well-intentioned, but neither can find a way out— a good option may be to agree to return to the subject at another time. When making this controlled freeze, it's advisable to "meta-communicate," which means spending a few moments talking about the communication process itself. For example, "We've been talking about this for half an hour, and I believe you want to find an agreement as much as I do. But we seem to be stuck. Could we pick it up again tomorrow?"

Although you should not often have to resort to controlled fight, flight, or freeze, it's essential to keep this possibility in mind. By doing so, you avoid an important source of stress: the self-imposed pressure to succeed at all costs. Unlike a football match, where the score is more important than the quality of the play, how you handle a difficult conversation supersedes the operational outcome. The idea is to return to dialogue without any injuries, and if this requires going to extra time, so be it!

Acknowledging the possibility of failure (temporary or definitive) has other advantages, too. Accepting that the candid exchange may fail to achieve calm allows you to focus more on the *process*. Although you care about the outcome of the exchange, of course, judging the quality of your efforts based on that outcome alone is a mistake. Sometimes, you may do everything humanly possible but fail, while on other occasions, you can make multiple communication errors but get lucky and succeed.

Also, it is a matter of common experience that when you don't put yourself under pressure to succeed, paradoxically, it's more likely that you will!

The four stances of a candid exchange

As you venture into a candid exchange, you might struggle with where to start. You feel the presence of the troll, and you hesitate, pondering the ghastly consequences of saying the wrong thing. There isn't one right way, but it helps if you consciously choose where to begin and remain aware of what you're doing throughout the exchange.

Hence, while describing a candid exchange, I find that it helps to discuss four separate aspects, or "stances": Pause, Ask, Listen, and Explain.

There is an overlap between the four. While pausing, for example, you're also asking, listening, and explaining *internally*. Mastering this internal dialogue is a prerequisite for managing a candid exchange.

When you read about the four parts of a candid exchange, I thus urge you to consider both the internal and external aspects of communication. How we talk to ourselves deserves the same discipline as communicating with others. Furthermore, how we communicate with others reflects what we tell ourselves. If we persecute ourselves with judgmental language, we will probably do the same to others. Conversely, if we talk to ourselves benevolently, we will probably do the same to others.

Whether or not you succeed in getting back to dialogue, candid exchanges are almost always worthwhile. Instead of trying to sneak past the troll, you are much better off when you accept some short-term discomfort and get to grips with him. Instead of adding another issue to your list of to-be-dealt-with-later problems, you engage in an intimate conversation with someone and create the possibility of getting to know them better.

Even if the exchange is less than successful, you'll probably learn something from it. You'll be able to better deal with your next troll or even the same one at a later date.

Pause

Pausing, you might have thought, would come naturally to anyone who encounters a troll. However, people often just plow straight into difficult conversations, relying on habit and instinct. The Pause step is thus crucial to control your feelings, gather your thoughts, and *consciously* decide what to do.

You must consider three things:

- What story are you telling yourself about this situation?
- What exactly is the difficulty?
- In addressing this difficulty, what is your fundamental intention?

Given the ambient emotional tension, you may find it difficult to remember the above, and you might find yourself making the following mistakes:

- Having a distorted view of the situation, thanks to filters and biases
- Subtly avoiding the real difficulty, not quite going to the heart of the matter
- Taking an unhelpful attitude, excessively focused on immediate results.

In this chapter, you'll learn about checking your story, moving toward the real difficulty, and deciding your intentions, thereby avoiding the pitfalls I just mentioned.

Check your story

The story you're telling yourself is part of your internal dialogue. Sometimes, it's a single, strong voice; at other times, it's a cacophony of contradicting thoughts. It may trigger a lot of difficult emotions, and if so, you need to ask yourself some questions.

For example, if you say to yourself something like, "This is unfair. They know how hard we worked!", you could ask, "Why do I believe this to be unfair?" and "How do I know what they're thinking?"

When you ask such questions, you are checking your filters and biases. You might then revise the story you're telling yourself to "This job was much harder than expected. Even so, we managed it! I wish they would show some appreciation for this."

Managing your internal conversation thus can help you calm down. It also prepares you for the rest of the candid exchange by "cleaning up" your thoughts. The more these thoughts align with the person you want to be and your intentions for this exchange (see below), it is more likely that both your verbal and nonverbal communication will flow naturally and be effective.

To quickly recognize the flaws in the story you're telling yourself, you must already have a solid understanding of your built-in filters and biases. These data processing tools you have built up over the years allow you to interpret new situations quickly. Unfortunately, they can also lead you to jump to conclusions that others disagree with, thereby creating a danger of conflict.

As I'll discuss, when you explain your viewpoint to someone, it's essential to present the relevant data accurately, separating opinion from fact. The same goes for your internal dialogue. You must recognize tyrannical assessments (see *Assessment tyranny*). If, for example, you find yourself thinking, "That's a ridiculous price!" you should realize that this is an opinion expressed as though it were a fact. Therefore, you must substitute it with something like, "I don't want to pay that much. About X euros would work for me."

A customer story

Suppose your customer asks about supply chain issues *again*, just as they did during the last meeting and the one before, and for as long as you can remember. As usual, they do this just when you get to important topics, and an agonized, apocalypse-is-nigh expression accompanies their question.

Much of what we've learned about dealing with difficult conversations is unintuitive. Since habit and instinct can't be relied upon, you know *not* to say the first thing that comes into your head. Instead, you ask yourself why you feel irritated.

Your emotional discomfort doesn't *directly* depend on outside stimuli, such as your customer's words and expressions. The sequence of events in the above example is the following:

1. You hear what is said and see telltale facial movements.
2. You assess what you've heard and seen.
3. Emotions stir inside you *in response to your assessment*.

Or, as Shakespeare's Hamlet concisely put it:

> *"Nothing's ever good or bad,*
> *But thinking makes it so."*

Hence, when your customer brings up supply chain issues and grimaces, you are frustrated, but *they are not the direct cause of that feeling*.

You are frustrated because of the *combination* of your observations and sensitivities.

Once something has happened or been said, it can't unhappen or be unsaid, so you can do nothing about that part of the equation. Hence, the key to remaining calm is to control the *story you tell yourself* about what you see and hear. It's *your* story; you are responsible for it and can choose a different one. You are in control, and it's up to you whether you stay in control.

Your story contains many subplots: your opinion of the customer and your joint project, your experience of similar situations, the amount of work you have on your plate, and so on.

In the case of your "irritating" customer, the first thing you say to yourself—the first draft of your story—might be as follows: "These guys have no idea how difficult it is for us Application Engineers. And why does he think that his company is so special? Whatever's wrong, it's not my fault!" Furthermore, the label that you have attributed to the customer—"irritating"—is also a part of your story.

The revised story goes something like this: "I guess he's under a lot of pressure from his management, like me. And we've been telling him that he's a special customer, so he probably doesn't understand why others are getting parts and not him. I can handle this." In addition, you stop labeling him "irritating."

This revision helps you relax and feel more comfortable. A further benefit is that it makes you less vulnerable to manipulation—many well-known, unscrupulous influencing techniques take advantage of how people think when gripped by emotions. If you were to become anxious that this customer would stop working with you—and this may be the reaction they're trying to provoke—then you'd be vulnerable to making concessions you'd not otherwise consider. Perhaps you'd promise to get them a larger discount on something or allocate free engineering support. The price of losing control of your emotions could then be pretty high.

> *A happy troll can also be a problem*
>
> *When discussing difficult conversations, it's normal to focus on the negative emotions—anger, fear, and sadness. But don't forget that joy can also be a problem.*
>
> *This is the Happy Troll Problem.*
>
> *When the atmosphere is one of uncontrolled enthusiasm, it's easy to make unwise decisions that entail unjustifiable risks. The*

> *situation is essentially the same as when there is an unhappy troll, and the challenge remains the same as well: getting back to calm dialogue.*
>
> *Of course, once the issue has been recognized, addressing it should be painless. For example, suppose your team wins a prize, and you see them euphoric and getting carried away; you might suggest the happy variant of a candid exchange—some kind of celebration to allow them an energy release. You might say, "Hey guys, we're all thrilled to get this prize. Let's take a break from our usual routine and talk about who and what made it all possible."*
>
> *Once everyone has enjoyed talking about their success, the happy troll leaves, and calm returns to the room. You may then return to serious operational issues.*

Distortions to watch out for

When cleaning up the story that you are telling yourself, look out for:

- Universal thinking errors
- Personal filters and biases.

Certain thinking errors are built into your DNA, and everyone is prone to them. As if that were not enough, you also have filters and biases that depend on your personality, your beliefs, and your life experiences.

Distortions: Universal thinking errors

Thinking errors (also known as cognitive biases) distort the story you tell yourself, increasing the chances of an emotional overreaction and making it even more difficult to achieve calm!

Being aware of your "favorite" thinking errors—the ones you most often succumb to—is an important aspect of self-understanding, as it allows you to correct your stories faster. Daniel Kahneman, a Nobel Prize winning psychologist, studied universal thinking errors closely and, with his colleagues, identified an impressive number of them (Kahneman). For example:

Confirmation bias creates blind spots that prevent you from understanding an issue. For example, believing a colleague's software to be buggy, you may interpret a system crash as proof that you are right—clearly it was caused by a bug that they introduced! This is probably a false story unlikely to enhance your relationship with your colleague.

Labeling is when you categorize yourself and others based on a generalization. For example, when your project goes wrong, you may label yourself as "a poor leader," even though there were many factors apart from your leadership that influenced the project outcome. Such a story erodes your self-confidence, hampers your leadership skills, and transforms the label into a self-fulfilling prophecy.

Emotional attribution error means thinking that somebody or something external to you is the cause of your uncomfortable feelings. Instead of attributing emotions to a combination of your observations and sensitivities, you blame a person or a thing. So, you may say to yourself or even out loud, "She's got me all upset!" or "He makes me feel depressed!" or "This software drives me nuts!"

The above example of your customer with supply chain problems showed how labelling can be combined with an emotional attribution error. In the sketch, by labeling the customer as "irritating", you were attributing the cause of your irritation to the customer rather than to the story you were telling yourself about the customer and the situation.

Thinking errors, unfortunately, pollute your internal dialogue and can lead to inappropriate words and actions.

> ### *Thinking error homework*
> *The catalog of universal thinking errors is huge. Try looking up some of the following:*

> - *The Sunk Cost Fallacy:* Ruminating about unrecoverable, already spent time and effort.
> - *The Availability Illusion:* Overestimating the probability of events because similar ones are easy to recall.
> - *Regression to the Mean:* An example of the brain's lack of intuition for statistical phenomena.

Distortions: Personal filters and biases

Your filters cause you to listen preferentially for certain types of information and to unconsciously exclude other types.

Positive filters make a preferential selection, and they do so at the expense of rejected but potentially valuable information. For example, some people listen mainly for *factual information*, others mostly for *opinions*. Some pick up feelings first, whereas others home in on *events*—they have an *action filter*. On the other hand, people with a *reaction* filter focus on likes and dislikes, while a few of us tune in best to *reflections and ideas*[12].

Dealing with positive filters does not involve eliminating them—instead, it involves augmenting them with other positive filters. For example, if you know that you preferentially hear facts, you should make a special effort to notice feelings and other types of information. Similarly, focusing on more abstract reflections and ideas might be a good idea if you tend to focus only on actions.

Negative filters cause you to unconsciously exclude information that doesn't fit your personal interests, your preferred writing/speaking style, and other criteria. This mechanism reduces the amount of information your conscious brain has to cope with. However, it may cause you to overlook important details. For example, you may ignore things that seem *familiar* and jump to hasty conclusions.

When computers first came into the home, I enjoyed creating games and considered myself familiar with the basics of game creation. Years later, when my kids were raving about the new, super cool fantasy games in their PlayStations, I filtered out almost everything they told me about those games. "The same old, same old," I told myself, sticking with my obsolete impression of computer games.

I had failed to see what was new and unfamiliar, and, as a result, I didn't understand my kids' enthusiasm for the new breed of entertainment. I had fallen into the familiarity trap created by my earlier game-writing experiences and years of working with computers.

Biases pick up where filters leave off. Despite your filters, some information gets through to your consciousness, where your personal biases then get to work, distorting your story with tyrannical assessments (see *Assessment tyranny*). Recall that you take the data from your filters, then make interpretations—hypotheses, deductions, projections, and so on. Having classified the resulting information, you evaluate it by applying rules and making judgments. While these evaluations simplify your story, allowing you a certain cognitive ease, the process causes further information loss. It compounds any errors introduced by the interpretations that preceded them.

Continuing the example above, my assessment of the computer games was further distorted by *confirmation bias*. I ignored any information contradicting my belief that my kids spent too much time in front of screens.

Biases and filters are closely related, and from a practical point of view, it is not vital to make a distinction. However, it's a good idea to develop an understanding of one's own.

When considering your "favorite" filters and biases, don't forget that they affect the assessment of both your outer and inner worlds. Confirmation bias often reinforces self-limiting appraisals, for example. Have you ever told yourself, "I am no good at X," while ignoring evidence to the contrary?

Empathy

You are only partly responsible for the troll in the room. Even if you manage to calm yourself completely, the room may still be emotionally charged by other people's feelings. It's obviously important to understand those feelings as well as you can, and to do this, you need empathy. You should try to figure out what the other party is seeing and experiencing, and then you might be able to imagine some of their feelings, too.

However, it's more complicated than that since, although everyone has a fairly similar emotional apparatus, you can't assume that others will assess what they see and experience in the same way as you would.

Recall the preceding discussion of distortions to look out for: thinking errors, filters, and biases. The other party's perspective will certainly suffer from all three of these distortions, but you don't know which thinking errors, filters, and biases they favor.

Based on this presentation of the problem, you might think that empathy is impossibly complicated. But don't give up yet, as you can develop your empathy skills by first applying them to yourself. In fact, you do this every time you check your story!

Getting used to examining your thoughts—your internal dialogue—and the feelings that they provoke will exercise the mental muscles you need to be empathetic towards others.

Your internal drama

Common or garden-variety thinking errors combine with your filters and biases and complicate your self-talk. So, you should forgive yourself if your story is not always right the first time.

I sometimes feel that there's a TV series playing in my head, with different characters arguing, vying for control, and taking the winner and loser roles in turn. Psychologically speaking, this is a useful description of what is going on, and this idea has been captured in a concept known as the "drama triangle." (Karpman) The triangle involves three roles—a Victim, a Persecutor, and a Rescuer—and the actors switch between these roles at crucial moments in the drama.

This model provides valuable insight into stress and the underlying thought processes. It also helps us understand how to better manage them. Essentially, the script of this internal drama is the story you're telling yourself, and its plot, like a theatre plot, is structured and predictable. It might go something like this:

Once upon a time, there was a victim. "Poor me, I've been working hard all week. It's Friday night, and my partner has just organized a crazy busy weekend. I've got to start renovating the bathroom tomorrow, go out to the Dixons in the evening, and, if there's any time left on Sunday, help with the tax return. Poor me, I think I'll have a drink. I deserve one or two."

This drama starts with you in the Victim role, and then, just before the break, when you offer yourself a compensatory drink, you switch to the Rescuer role (rescuing yourself, of course).

The drama resumes the next morning when you wake up with a hangover. "You idiot!" you tell yourself. "Why can't you keep yourself under control? It's always like this."

Here, you've woken up in the Persecutor role, feeling irritable and giving yourself a hard time.

You might then go on to injure yourself while attacking the bathroom DIY, becoming a Victim once again, then perhaps a Rescuer, should you decide to give yourself a break and watch football instead of working.

You should know you have an internal drama when you notice the repetitive role-switching pattern illustrated in the above example. You will perhaps sense confusion and discomfort as you switch between the three roles, alternately feeling anxiety, righteous anger, and indulgent self-pity. Once you have recognized this, you are in a stronger position to break out of the triangle.

You do so by talking to yourself in an adult fashion, doing your best to assess the facts and feelings of the situation, and checking how you have filtered, interpreted, and evaluated them. All being well, you'll come to reasonable conclusions and make conscious decisions about what to do. It may still involve watching football instead of replumbing the bathroom, but now you can do so without feeling guilty.

Address the real difficulty

You avoid the difficulty at the heart of a conversation for three main reasons:

- Failure to notice the issue
- Failure to understand the issue
- Apprehension.

The difficulty at the heart of a conversation may seem obvious to you, but sometimes, this means that you jump to conclusions and fail to notice the real issue. Alternatively, you may see that there is a non-trivial problem to deal with, but you can't fully understand it. Finally, you might notice and understand the issue, either consciously or subconsciously, but recognizing its thorny nature, you turn away and tackle something less fearful instead.

Whatever the underlying issue is, it must be recognized and, when possible, acted upon. Dealing promptly with such difficulties helps avoid a build-up of issues that pollute relationships.

Failure to notice

For example, suppose Chris turns up late for your team's weekly meeting. You might have one of the following reactions:

- You wave the issue aside with a "No problem, Chris!"
- You confront him with a "Chris, this meeting started at 10 am, and it is now quarter past 10… "
- You pause to think.

After you pause for thought, you might realize that the real problem is that Chris is invariably late. You fear that they respect neither you nor their colleagues. Hence, instead of dismissing the issue or confronting him, you might decide to take Chris aside after the meeting and have a candid exchange about motivation and accountability.

This example highlights a common phenomenon: an obvious problem (someone arriving late for a meeting) masking a more important one (a lack of respect).

Failure to understand

When trying to understand a non-trivial problem, it can help to look at it from the perspectives of power, trust, and value. These factors are often at the heart of a communication problem—they are the real difficulties—and it's vital to recognize them through the fog of operational activities.

In the above case, the operational activity is the weekly meeting, and the superficial issue is that Chris turned up late. However, you recognized that the real difficulty was probably that Chris did not *value* you (as their manager) or your colleagues.

Other people in the meeting might have taken a different point of view. One of Chris' colleagues might have been saying to themselves, "Who does he think he is? Waltzing in here like he owns the place! I'm just as important as him!" For this person, the real difficulty is one of *power*.

Someone else might have asked themselves if they could *trust* Chris with project responsibilities, given that he invariably turns up late for meetings.

Now, let's revisit the "irritating" customer case at the start of this chapter and try to understand why they are worked up. On the surface, the problem is that we're not supplying them with components on time. Is this the core issue, or is it one of power? Perhaps they want us to treat them as a top-priority customer but are frustrated because we have control over who we serve first.

Perhaps trust is the issue. If they believe we told them they were a key customer, a strategic account, a valued business partner, and so on, and then, when the wind changes, they find that they are no more important to us than any other client, then their trust in us will have taken a bashing.

Finally, you may look at the case through the lens of value: do they think their company doesn't matter to us? Suppose we are dealing with a small startup passionate about their niche solution for water recycling. Suppose they find it hard to be heard in the battle for the exploding market in eco-friendly solutions. They may think that we overlooked them and that, for us, they are unimportant compared to established companies.

Pinpointing difficulties is not the only use of the perspectives of power, trust, and value. You can also use them to question the story you're telling yourself. In the example we've been working with, the first version of your story was, "Once again, I have to deal with an unhappy customer." However, thinking about this from a power perspective, you see that *they may be using supply chain problems to divert attention away from other topics*. Perhaps they are not upset but manipulative, attempting to take control of the agenda with this ploy. They could be using it to avoid talking about their own shortcomings or to cover something up. You need to find out, and this changes your intentions for the candid exchange.

Apprehension

Failing to notice or understand an issue can also be associated with apprehension. Your underlying distress when faced with lack of respect, for example, may augment your preference for a simpler but more superficial way of dealing with the situation. If this is so, you are driven by the subconscious, and your apprehension needs some time to take shape and be recognized. Hence, once again, you see that pausing for thought is extremely important when you detect emotional discomfort. It will allow you to analyze your apprehension.

Apprehension is always related to some kind of fear, whether it be the fear of something real, such as a poor performance rating, or anticipated, such as the *possibility* of a poor performance rating. The latter type of fear is called anxiety or worry, and if they're the problem, then you should go right back to the previous guideline: "Check your story." What are you saying to yourself that provokes an anxious feeling? Does the reality of your situation justify such a feeling? How certain are you of the data driving this story?

Let's assume that, having checked your story, you find a real cause for concern. There is a possibility that, if you don't handle this situation correctly, the result might be conflict, embarrassment, or collateral damage. Rather than facing these perils, it's tempting to politely work around them, to perhaps hint at a profound issue but not address it directly.

Of course, this is a highly inefficient and ineffective way to proceed!

Although facing an issue head-on may be difficult and uncomfortable, the alternatives are dismal. Swallowing feelings—smiling despite pain and distress, craving the approval of everyone around—leads to a sort of emotional indigestion. And forever changing subjects to avoid critical issues gets exhausting, as you often have to find cumbersome and indirect solutions to problems you should tackle head-on.

Furthermore, avoiding an issue leaves you alone with your fears, whereas tackling that issue allows you to see if those fears are well-founded. While avoidance offers you a temporary break, it does not allow you to build resilience. Nor does it allow you to develop your difficult conversation skills and improve your confidence.

But perhaps the worst thing about avoidance is that it makes matters worse. The people affected by a festering issue do not forget about it, so when you finally get around to dealing with the problem, you find that it has grown bigger than ever.

Problems only get solved when you address them.

Adjust your intentions

Now that you have had a chance to examine your story and identify the real difficulty, you must adjust your intention toward the other party, aligning it with your updated strategy and expectations. By doing this, you put yourself in a position to deal with the unexpected and recover from any mistakes you

may make when communicating. If you neglect to do this, your communication, however technically correct, cannot achieve the result you're hoping for. Your intention is the port you will steer toward, adjusting your sails as the conversation blows first one way and then another. With this port to aim for, you can be confident of finding a way through whatever storms may appear.

An intention is an expression of purpose. In this context, it explains *why* you want a candid exchange. You know that you have clarified your intention once you have captured it in a word or two, and you feel comfortable about explaining it to the other party if needed.

There is often no need to communicate your intention explicitly, as people pick up on verbal and non-verbal signals, rendering explanations unnecessary. However, this is not always the case, and it is better to be safe than sorry. If you even slightly suspect that your intentions have been misunderstood, then you could try saying, for example, "Would it help if I explained why I want to talk to you about this?"

This is an example of meta-communication, mentioned in an earlier chapter. Meta-communication takes a little time but quickly pays off—like organizing one's desk before starting work for the week.

However, whether you state your intention explicitly or not, you first have to formulate it. The rest of this subsection suggests guidelines for doing this.

Useful intentions for a candid exchange

You can capture your intentions in a few words. These "anchors" must be short and simple, allowing you to fix them in your mind.

Here are a few examples of intentions you might carry into a candid exchange:

- Prevent/clarify/understand (something)
- Support/reassure/listen to (a person or a group)
- Energize/encourage/amuse (a person or a group).

Bear in mind that the objective of the candid exchange is always to achieve calm (i.e. to get the troll out of the room), so your intention must be in the service of that objective. For example: "Prevent further speculation and worry,"; "Clarify the memo,"; "Understand their complaint,"; "Reassure them that X is a priority," and "Encourage her to share her ideas."

Well-adjusted intentions, understood by all parties, have almost magical powers. When unexpected obstacles trash your careful meeting preparation, you can work around them if you know where you want to get to. As mentioned, they are a port to steer toward. When you mess up and get lost, clear intentions help you get back on course.

In the example we have been following, you suspect the customer may be using your supply chain problems to divert your attention away from other topics. You could, therefore, engage in a candid exchange with the intention of understanding their motives.

Notice that this is quite different from the intention you might have had if, because of their complaints, you had jumped to the conclusion that late deliveries were the only issue. In this case, your intention might have simply been to reassure them of your best efforts.

Even worse, if you'd not paused for thought at all, your reaction might have been fueled by irritation. Intent on defending your position, you could have started by deriding the customer's remarks: "As I believe I have explained a couple of times now, ..." The customer might not appreciate this kind of sarcasm, a direct result of the maladjusted intention.

On the other hand, trust increases when one's intentions are correctly adjusted and the other party understands them. Trust signals that people accept each other's intentions, believing them to be compatible with their needs.

Several years ago, I had a series of difficult conversations with a long-term customer. They'd badly messed up their accounts and called to ask that I withdraw several invoices, essentially crediting back a large sum of money that was legally mine.

This was a giant troll. On my customer's side, serious cashflow issues might entail irreversible consequences. On my side, my family was in no mind to accept the potential financial loss.

It might have ended very badly if both sides had not clearly intended to find a solution that would allow our business to recover and continue. Despite the messy communication, we could both see that the other was doing their best under difficult circumstances and that neither of us was attempting to profit from the situation. This generated sufficient trust for us to work something out despite the technical errors in communication.

All the checklists in the world would not have helped us. This experience reinforced my belief in the importance of intention over technique.

Intentions versus objectives

Intention statements are more abstract than those generally used for operational objectives, which tend to be more detailed and context-dependent.

For example, while your intention for a candid exchange might be simply "Listen to him," your objectives when you venture into a complex discussion could include the following:

1. Understand which technology to use (20 nanometer, if possible).
2. Get agreement on the use of our Non-Disclosure Agreement.
3. Decide the project lead and the start date (next quarter).

An artificial intelligence tool may have objectives, but it certainly does not have intentions since a machine cannot (yet) understand the purpose of what it is doing. Only mindful, sentient beings can have intentions. An artificial intelligence engine can write a book about a given topic in a particular style, but it does not know what the text means.

To reiterate, you may have operational objectives for a difficult conversation, but your only aim for the candid exchange within it is to reach calm—to have the troll leave the room. Once calm is achieved, you may address the operational objectives.

Consider Aesop's fable of the hare and the tortoise with a minor change: instead of a race, the two animals are engaged in a difficult conversation. The hare is in a big hurry, tearing along, intent on reaching its ultimate goal, while the tortoise tortoise sets out only with the aim of having a candid exchange, which will lead to calm. The tortoise realizes that, once the candid exchange is done, it will be able to discuss whatever the hare's worried about easily enough. We all know whose strategy is more effective.

Returning to the human race, imagine, for example, that you have an annual review with a team member, and your objectives for the conversation are, first, to let them know the poor grades you are giving them and, second, to discuss the reasons and start to work on an improvement plan with them.

We might expect things to heat up when the grades are discussed. If this happens—suppose that the team member gets angry, considers the poor grades unfair, and anticipates consequences for their salary, for example—then it would be a mistake to immediately pursue the other objectives. Even discussing the reasons for the grades would probably lead to an argument. The first thing to do is calm the troll (the emotion, resistance, or argumentativeness that has arisen).

An appropriate intention for this candid exchange might be to *reassure* your team member that you value their work and that you're doing your best to treat them fairly.

Intentions to prevail or manipulate

If you enter a candid exchange with the intention of prevailing or manipulating, you will likely end up with a Win-Lose or Lose-Win outcome. However, anything but a Win-Win rarely makes sense in business, as relationships between colleagues and companies generally rely on interdependence. Managers and leaders depend on their team members for expertise, advice, and even motivation. Big companies depend on much smaller ones for various products and services. The idea that a manager-leader can win at the expense of their team or that a customer can run roughshod over their suppliers does not make sense in this world of complex relationships.

To avoid inadvertently adopting intentions that, when examined closely, can be seen as domineering or manipulative, it helps to understand their origins and how they show up in practice.

The intention to prevail[1] is motivated by the need to dominate (Perel, "What Couples Therapy Can Teach Us"). For example, intending to prove you are right (and that someone else is wrong) or to show that you're clever (and that others are less so). Fundamentally, it is about power, a topic already visited earlier in this chapter.

Although you do not like it when you sense intentions to prevail in another person, you may sometimes be guilty of them yourself. Consider these cases:

- When you feel affronted or embarrassed by "constructive" feedback received in public, you want to get your own back. This is called revenge.
- Driven by a strong sense of right and wrong, you insist on your opinion being heard. That is called crusading.
- Conditioned by a culture that highly values success, you need to assert yourself forcefully. This is called warmongering.
- Proud of the quality and correctness of your ideas, you wish to explain your solution. This is called showing you're right.

These examples show how you can easily stray into counterproductive territory. In each case, the origin of the intention is ordinary and legitimate: the discomfort of embarrassment, strong beliefs, an inherited culture, and a commitment to quality. You must, therefore, recognize when you've transformed such a stimulus into an unhelpful intention.

An intention to manipulate is also associated with a strong need for control over the other party: your customer, boss, or team member, for example. Driven by this need, you try to influence others to do or say things contrary to their interests (that they would not do if they were aware of being manipulated).

This manipulative approach is counterproductive. Of course, nobody likes being tricked, and when they recognize the manipulation, the relationship suffers.

Consider an example inspired by actual events. A company has delivered a software product, but it has discovered that the product has some expensive-to-fix bugs.

At a meeting with their clients to discuss some new urgent feature requests, rather than admit that they have discovered bugs in their software, they decide to take advantage of the client's need for new features. They agree to nearly all their requests on the condition that the client increases the project budget. *Unknown to the client,* the company will use this extra money to fix their bugs.

Rather than manipulating their client this way, getting them to provide funding without revealing how it will be used, a better-adjusted intention would be to create an atmosphere where all the issues and requirements—including the bug—could be discussed constructively. Such an intention would likely lead to an open and honest, though robust, exchange, with a good chance of a Win-Win outcome.

Pausing is not hesitating

When I think of the times I have been conversing with people who have the confidence to pause for thought when they need to, I remember how impressed I have been. Thomas d'Ansembourg[14], a leader of the Non-Violent Communication movement, is a case in point. Although he is phenomenally fluent and can hold an audience spellbound with his lucidity and speed of thought, he simply stops when he needs to. Rather than being puzzled or feeling embarrassed, his students tend to be extremely impressed—this capability definitely adds to his stage presence!

On the other hand, the absence of white space in a conversation is a problem. Conversing with someone anxious to fill any silence and who jumps at the chance to take the speaking role irritates me. I get the impression they are not listening to what I'm saying. Instead, they seem preoccupied with pushing a pre-prepared argument.

It is okay to pause for thought, and this chapter has given you some ideas about how you can best use the space a pause creates. When you pause, you calm down, identify the difficulty you need to address, and decide on your intentions. When you manage this, you silently influence the other parties of the conversation, which then becomes more authentic and worthwhile.

So, don't hesitate to pause!

Ask

Questions shape and determine the flow of a conversation. How you ask the other party to contribute to a conversation is thus crucial.

Consider what happens when you ask, "Why do you think that's true?" This question steers the exchange and, perhaps, encourages the other party to consider something they hadn't given much thought to previously.

Since asking is a powerful tool, it is worth spending some time fully understanding its features and figuring out how to use them skillfully. To start with, there is the channel to consider. Think of this as the other party's preferred wavelength. If you can tune into this, they will hear you much better. Then, there is the request itself and, finally, the capacity of the other person to respond. Your asking tool, if used well, can help them give a response that moves the exchange forward.

These three aspects of asking are reflected in the guidelines of our hero's thought bubble in the picture above, which will be discussed shortly. In addition, we'll look at the wide range of things you can achieve through asking. This device can be used for questioning, of course. In addition, you can use asking to invite others to contribute to an exchange or solicit them to do things. Each of these three types of asking—enquiring, inviting, and soliciting—has its own subtle characteristics, as we'll see.

Use the right channel

As I just mentioned, you may use different channels (or asking styles, if you prefer)[15].

Suppose your colleagues are on edge, and you try to lighten up the atmosphere with a cheerful "And so, last but not least, and always good for a few new ideas, let's hear from Miko!" If Miko is inclined toward playfulness, this approach may work well. However, if they are serious by nature, using this playful channel could result in a sarcastic backlash.

It is important not only *what* you ask but also *how* you ask it. For example, there's a difference between the following asks:

1. "Tell me what you think!"
2. "What's your opinion?"
3. "And so I'm guessing that you've got a view on this too!?" (smiling)
4. "Now, I know that this topic is something that you care about, and I want you to feel included in this process, so please, can you tell me what you think?"

The four basic channels

Each of us has a natural default style, which generally works well, at least during calm dialogue. However, when emotions are running high, and the person you are talking to seems stressed, you must make more efforts to adapt your style to theirs. Some prefer to receive a simple and respectful directive, such as, "Tell me what you think!" They will then respond in a straightforward, adult way, and when they do so, you will know that you chose the right channel.

Others prefer a question—"What's your opinion?"—and, again, you'll get the confirmation that this is the right channel if they respond with a straightforward answer (rather than with another question, joke, or complaint, for example).

Some people favor a less "serious" channel. They enjoy contact with others and tend to be playful. In this case, the third channel—"And so I'm guessing..."—is more effective. It gives them the freedom to respond creatively and to inject some zest into the proceedings. However, the underlying message is the same as in the first two cases.

Finally, the fourth channel is preferred by people who strongly need a personal touch. Their first thoughts are about people and relationships, and they are less concerned with projects, ideas, and data. Their preferred communication style reflects this bias.

The Process Communication Model (PCM) has identified the following channels (brackets contain examples):

- Directive ("Send me the presentation tonight, please!")
- Requestive ("Can you send me the presentation tonight, please?")
- Emotive ("You'll send it before you go for a beer tonight, right?")
- Nurturing ("It would be nice if you could send me the presentation tonight")

When using the *directive* channel, you make a direct request with an imperative. As with all the channels, you may use this one gently, politely, and respectfully. When you use the directive channel, you take a protective posture, providing the other person with unambiguous information about what you expect. There is nothing else for them to do but follow or not follow your directions. Despite its natural association with the word "director," the use of this channel does not imply superiority—it's simply a way of communicating. Some people prefer it when making a request, and some people prefer it when receiving a request.

People taking a neutral position favor the *requestive* channel. This position contrasts with the protective or encouraging parent associated with the directive and nurturing channels and with the playful child of the emotive one. The requestive channel favors a crisp and polite exchange of information.

The *emotive* channel is playful and energizing, ideally suited to animate groups. Like the other channels, it can still be gentle, polite, and respectful while injecting a little spice into the conversation. Being playful does not mean teasing.

Finally, the *nurturing* channel is associated with the part of the personality that expresses caring and seeks to hearten another person. Therefore, the messages sent with this channel typically contain more "feeling words" and verbs in the conditional.

Consider what happens when someone who prefers a directive style of communication receives a nurturing message. They may ask themselves, "Why don't they just say what they want?!" Similarly, if you like to be playful and prefer emotive messages, you will likely react to a straightforward request with "What's wrong with them today?" Finally, someone who puts feelings before other considerations will prefer a nurturing channel, and a simple directive may prompt the thought, "Why don't they care about me?"

Given that your favored channel is not a universal preference, you must be prepared to make an extra effort. You must match the other party's default received channel with your transmit channel, even if it is not your favorite. If you fail to do this, both of you will be on different wavelengths, and if the receiver does not have the energy or inclination to tune into your frequency, the communication will be poor.

Adaptation exercise

PCM has six fundamental personality types at its core, and each of us is a hybrid of all of them. The four channels presented here are each associated with one or more personality types, but

> *since you are a cross of all these types, you can use all four! To do this, you need to become familiar with each channel and develop the dexterity to switch to any one of them. When you do so, you will be in a stronger position to understand the channels other people prefer and switch to them when necessary.*
>
> *As an exercise, the next time you think about something to ask someone, try expressing your message with each of the four PCM channels the next time you think about something to ask someone. Write down your ideas and rewrite them until each seems as natural as possible.*

On the wrong wavelength

You must not assume that the other party has the same communication preferences as you. The following story of a couple on a long drive beautifully illustrates this mistake (Perel, "Relational Intelligence"):

"Would you like to stop for a drink, darling?"

"No, thanks," replies the driver.

A long, awkward silence descends on the pair.

When they can bear it no longer, the driver asks, "What's wrong?"

"Nothing."

"I don't believe you. You were chatting away normally for an hour and then suddenly went silent 10 minutes ago."

"Yes, well, I wanted to stop for a drink."

"Then why didn't you say so?"

"I did!"

"You didn't! You asked me if I wanted to stop."

"Yes, and you don't understand anything!"

In this case, the driver's default communication channel is either directive or requestive—it is hard to figure it out from the dialogue. However, their partner prefers a *nurturing* (and somewhat indirect) channel. Hence, the driver takes the question, "Would you like to stop for a drink?" at face value, not understanding that it is a solicitation to stop.

Language analogy

To get an idea of what it's like to receive a message on alternative channels, consider :

1. Can you send me the presentation tonight, please?
2. Schick mir bitte die Präsentation heute Abend!
3. Il serait sympa si tu pourrais m'envoyer la presentation ce soir.
4. Lo invierai prima di andare a bere una birra stasera, vero?

Depending on your knowledge of different European languages, you'll find some of these messages easier to interpret than others. Furthermore, if you are in a hurry and under stress, the first version may be the only one you can respond to.

Communication channels are like languages in many ways. You have a default, favored language and may understand others. As you go through life, you may become adept at more languages, but you will certainly prefer your default one, especially when you are tired or under stress. This language metaphor suggests that the more you practice using different channels, the more fluent you become in them.

Just ask

The "Just ask" idea encourages straightforwardness and discourages prevarication. It also invites you to ask without undue delay: to switch to the asking stance early during the exchange and switch back to it frequently thereafter.

When explaining something before asking for a response, keep it as brief and simple as possible. If you are too wordy, the other party may stop listening and even miss your request.

To achieve the above, the following habits are particularly helpful:

- Remove anything superfluous
- Be comfortable with imperfection
- Use the present tense as much as possible

Remove anything superfluous

Unless you are talking to an angel, fully equipped with a harp, wings, and infinite patience, other people are much more focused on their concerns than on what you are saying. They are not necessarily selfish, but evolution crafted every living thing on Earth for survival and to constantly ask, "What's in it for me?"

Also, your clients and colleagues have short attention spans, though it's not always been this way (Nutshell). In the past, when there were fewer distractions than nowadays, dazzling, verbose descriptions and flowery explanations helped people fill the long hours. It allowed them to overcome the existential void they must have felt in those dark times before TV, email, and social media. As Philippe (the illustrator of this book) pointed out to me, 19th-century writers were often paid by the line. Dickens and Zola made good money by churning out wonderfully long descriptive texts. In the 18th century, commuting between the Old World and the New, Benjamin Franklin regaled his companions with many a long anecdote before settling down to while away the long evenings, writing essays on every subject under the sun. In the early 20th century, Lawrence of Arabia's days were 99% camels, sand, and sun, even though the remaining 1% was so incredibly strange and exciting that he was able to write the Seven Pillars of Wisdom. This book is at least three times longer than its modern equivalents. These days, he'd be asked to capture his message in a tweet.

You might have been wondering when that last paragraph would finish! "So what? Get on with it!" I could hear you saying.

My point is that these days, we must not be long-winded, as I was above.

Hence, a request must be short, and the preamble to it must be either short or nonexistent. The purpose of the preamble is to help the other person better understand your request. It might clarify your intent, vocabulary, or context. For example:

- "I want to help you to..."
- "I'd like to understand..."
- "I'd like to ask you a question about X where, by X, I mean..."
- "Given that Y happened, why/how, etc...."

Leave out the non-essential stuff:

- Focus on the present situation (instead of the history of your problems).
- Put your worries aside. The other party does not need to know about your fears and fantasies.
- Control your curiosity, asking only questions that elicit vital information or prompt the other party to reflect.
- Only tell jokes and anecdotes if you think they will speed up progress.

In a nutshell, you should ask yourself before speaking, *"Will this help?"* If what you're about to explain or ask is unlikely to move things forward, do not say it.

In case you are worried that you'll lose control if you abstain from all but essential comments, remember that by letting the other party do most of the talking, you do not give up on shaping the conversation —quite the opposite. By asking questions and then "stepping back," you're guiding the exchange. You're structuring the conversation, influencing the other party's thoughts, and harvesting valuable information.

For example, if you explain to someone about enabling team performance and how to develop their team members' autonomy, they may glaze over. But if you ask, "Which options did you leave to your team when asking them for X?" they may stop to think! Your question sets the agenda for their thoughts and, hence, for your exchange.

In contrast, if you talk a lot, then you're sure to be interrupted, and each interruption allows the other party to take the conversation in the direction *they* want.

For all such reasons, waste no time before encouraging the other party to speak.

Strive for imperfection

Instead of trying to formulate the perfect request, allow yourself to make the occasional mistake when asking. Sometimes, things do not come out quite right—and that is okay.

You should strive for imperfection because perfectionism tends to produce hesitation, repetition, and verbosity. Struggling to ask for *exactly* what you need, you tend to slow your speech, perhaps introducing long pauses. Then, when the other party senses a chance to respond, you may even cut them off, reformulating your request to clarify an important point!

Worse still, you might add new requests to the original. These unwanted additions not only drag out the question and make it difficult to understand but also give the other party an out. If you ask three questions at once, they can pick the easiest one, avoiding the other two. Supposing that one of these two is critical, you missed an opportunity to address it.

When I think of the number of times I have to write a sentence before it comes out right, I wonder why I sometimes strive for perfect prose in the heat of a difficult conversation. If it takes me half a day to perfect one written sentence, how can I hope to get each spoken word perfectly right?

Sometimes, you can lose sleep, overthinking what you will say to someone the next day. When the time comes, you may slow your speech, afraid to say anything wrong, sounding like a broken tape recorder.

In my experience, the people who have the most success in difficult conversations are *not* the ones who produce impeccable requests—they are the ones who give others the maximum opportunities to respond.

Make the most of the present tense

By framing a request in the present, you make it easier for the other party to decide whether to comply. Using the present tense tends to result in simple, understandable, and non-threatening requests. In the context of a candid exchange, I highly recommend this practice.

When you ask using the present tense, there is no contract on the table. The other party does not have to be concerned about any future implications behind your request, and they don't have to worry about committing to something they'll later regret.

Furthermore, by using the present tense, you tend to employ positive terminology, in contrast to the negative terms often used when requesting something for the future. Consider this example: "Please don't send me your weekly report on a Friday evening ever again!" The team member who agreed to this request did not send their report at all if they did not get it done by the end of the week. This outcome was certainly not what the requester had in mind. However, since negative asks open many possibilities, the team member cannot be accused of breaking the agreement!

Finally, it's *easier for you* to use the present tense, as it's the most straightforward one. You'll make fewer mistakes when you favor it over more complicated grammar.

Free the response

When asking, you should do so in a way that makes the other party feel free to respond as they wish. The corollary to this idea is that you must accept their response for what it is, even if they decide not to reply. Silence, as we'll see, is a valid response.

Cornering

It's crucial to *ensure that the other person does not feel cornered*. Suppose you ask someone, "Please either agree or suggest another solution," and they strongly disagree with my proposal. If they can't think of a better alternative, they're stuck[16]. When you back an animal into a corner, it fights. So, this cornering request will likely result in conflict.

Cornering is often done with closed questions, such as, "Do you want it or not?" However, it is perfectly possible to corner someone with a question that is not closed. Consider, for example, the following:

1. "Why is it always my fault?"
2. "Why can't you ever just support me?"
3. "So, do you agree that's a fair summary?"
4. "You're the project lead, so what's your suggestion?"

The first two questions are cornering because it's almost impossible to answer them without falling into an argument.

The third example forces the person answering either to consent or to disagree, neither of which may be agreeable to them. A more reasonable ask might be, "So, what do you think of the summary?"

The fourth question obliges someone to take responsibility for solving the problem under discussion. A less cornering question might be, for example, "What do you think?" It's one of my favorites.

Remember also that, in a face-to-face situation, it's not just what's said that counts—physical positioning is important as well. So, it's a good idea not to block the way to the door! Human animals still have all their old instincts regarding escape routes and don't like to feel physically cornered.

Different channels to free the response

Here are some examples of how to give the other party the liberty to react as they wish, each using a different channel (see above for an explanation of channels).

If you decide to be directive, you might say, "Please consider what I said. I am interested in your immediate reaction, but take your time if you need to."

On the other hand, with a more nurturing style, you could ask, "I know that this may have been difficult to hear, and I want you to know that you have my full support. Are you able to talk about this with me now, or would you like some time to reflect?"

With a requestive style, you could say, "So, there are the facts. What do you think? 'No need to answer right away."

Finally, using a playful, emotive approach, you could ask the same thing in the following way: "Another day, another headache, eh? :-) When you've taken your paracetamol and feel up to it, let's talk some more. Or straight away, if you like...."

As mentioned at the beginning of this section, having given the other party space to choose their response, you must accept their choice. They may respond in a way that you object to or not respond at all, but you must not deny how they choose to react. Their reaction informs you about their state of mind. Considering this, you may then wish to pause to decide how to continue.

Frequently asked questions

Why don't they simply answer my questions?

The following example illustrates what can happen when the guidelines for asking are abused. Suppose I have a black sheep in my software development team. I am disappointed by their inability to think for themselves and take ownership of the projects assigned to them. When a small thing goes wrong, they wait for someone else to tell them what to do—or, even worse, they expect others to take over from them.

I thought about this and decided to talk to them about autonomy at work openly and honestly. So, the next time we had a one-on-one, I asked, "Hey, I've been thinking about your work style and would like to understand more about how you see your responsibilities. You're a bit younger than me, so perhaps we see things differently. I mean, in my first job...." I gave a couple of anecdotes, then continued, "... and so I was wondering where you see the boundaries. Do you agree that the responsibility for your projects lies with you at the end of the day?"

"Uh, I don't know. What do you mean?" they muttered, looking very uncomfortable.

"Well, do you see that, since you are the lead for the XYZ project, you will have to find a way to finish it on time?"

"Er, I suppose so."

"So, if we take this project of yours..."

I narrowed the interrogation down to areas where I believed they most needed to improve until, when the pressure got too much, they cracked.

"I don't know. I don't know. You tell me. I'm doing my best. It's difficult, that's all. I'll think about it. Is that all for now?" They got up and left.

"Blast!" I said to myself, "What did I say that was so wrong?"

Quite a lot, as we'll see.

For starters, I adopted an inquisitive approach and did not alter my tactics when it should have been apparent, after a couple of attempts, that they were not working. I should have changed channel, dropped the requestive style, and tried an alternative.

Second, I was far too verbose. The preamble to my opening question did not help matters at all!

Third, I did not accept or account for my team member's responses. Rather, I continued with my initial strategy, pinning them down and making the point I'd previously decided.

While the sketch is an invention, it is not completely fictional. As a young team leader working under pressure, I tended to micromanage and transmit my stress to my team members, and this is what's happening here. Anxious to get the black sheep to work as I expect them to, I tried to corner them with my questioning, thus imposing my beliefs and way of working on them.

Are you asking or demanding?

In my exchange with the black sheep, I acted like an enthusiastic Collie dog, herding my unlucky team member into a small pen, giving them no room to maneuver.

However, an office conversation is not a sheepdog trial, and the other party can refuse to be penned in, as they did in this case, by withdrawing from the conversation. Alternatively, they could have reacted angrily, standing up for themselves, defending their actions, and demanding better treatment from me. They could also have frozen, continuing with responses such as, "Er, I suppose so..." until the exchange fizzled out.

In all these cases, the resulting frustration and awkwardness would have been the result of my poorly formed requests. In fact, they were not requests but demands (Rosenberg).

When the other party hears a demand, their instincts take them in one of three directions: fight, flight, or freeze[17]. Since you do not want to force them down any of these paths, you must take care to make a genuine request, allowing space for a range of responses.

In *The Art of War*, San Tzu wrote thus: "Build your enemies a golden bridge." In other words, don't corner your adversary because people who feel trapped will fight to the death.

In a peacetime context, we would say that people who feel threatened and lack control will become aggressive and/or defensive, or they may withdraw (uncontrolled, instinctive fight, flight, or freeze responses). A "golden bridge" could mean some kind of choice, an acceptable compromise, or an honorable way out of a situation.

What are the different types of ask?

Just as the Inuit distinguishes between many types of snow, those interested in challenging conversations should distinguish between different types of ask and have the necessary vocabulary to describe these types.

When an ask follows an explanation, it's usually an *invitation* to respond with comments or questions. However, if you've just paused or finished listening, your ask is more likely to be an *inquiry* to the other party or a *solicitation* for them to do something.

Here are some examples:

- Invitation: "What do you think?"
- Inquiry: "When did you get to the office on Tuesday?"
- Solicitation: "Could we open the file and look at it together?"

Each type has particular characteristics, which I'll discuss in a moment:

- An *invitation* to respond may be much shorter than the two other types of request.
- An *inquiry* is made using Discovery skills, which many professionals already possess.
- A *solicitation* is most likely to be a Connection Request (see below).

Invitations

Perhaps surprisingly, clarity is not always a top priority when asking, especially when you are inviting someone to contribute their ideas to an exchange. An imprecise invitation does not constrain the other party to a particular type of response, and they may appreciate this freedom. Hence, ambiguity can even be beneficial.

I do a lot of coaching and work in two languages. Exactness is not my greatest strength, even in my mother tongue, but I am amazed that I get by using my second language. With my accent, my broken vocabulary, and my erratic use of verbs, it's a miracle that my clients stick with me. However, my success and failure rates are the same in both languages.

I believe this is because the quality of expression is far less important than the quality of listening. I've noticed that people frequently only half-listen to what I ask and that their replies are largely determined by whatever was on their minds before I spoke. What I ask or say often doesn't matter so much.

For this reason, I have stopped worrying about being eloquent, and although I do my best to ask clearly, I rarely correct a request if it comes out wrong. I do that only when the other party clearly needs guidance and is struggling to understand what I have asked.

Since you don't always have to make your invitation precise, simply prompting or nudging the other party can be sufficient. Often, your main goal is to have them express themselves and understand what they are thinking and feeling. One way you can do this, for example, is to ask yourself a question, speaking to yourself quietly but audibly. For example, "I'm wondering if this isn't something we should sleep on..."; "Perhaps there's some history I don't know about..."; "Maybe I need to talk to....". The almost irresistible temptation to complete these sentences can make the invitations very effective!

Another way is to wait expectantly or gently nudge with phrases such as "And so...?" or "And you...?"

This works particularly well after you've shared your observations, feelings, or needs because the other party is usually impatient to respond. Either way, you lose nothing by trying a gentle nudge, and you can always fall back on something more explicit, such as the following:

- "Having listened to what I just said, what are your thoughts?"
- "Would you tell me how you feel about what I just said?"

Inquiries

You may enquire just to find something out or to get the other person talking. By encouraging them to explain something, you may help them master their emotions and perhaps start to see things differently. Remember that the purpose of a candid exchange is to get to a calm, professional conversation, so your shaping efforts must go in this direction. The other party may find that explaining their point of view helps them relax. It might even lead to a resolution of the issue at hand (Betts, chapters 5 and 6).

On the other hand, if your inquiry is a request for information, then having discovery skills is helpful. You should delay extensive discovery until you return to dialogue, but a few discovery questions may be beneficial. In this case, it helps to remember that discovery is all about *exploration*. Rather than ask pointed and obvious questions about the difficulty right in front of you, you can learn about the other people and things that are influencing your situation[18]. Beyond finding out who and what these influences may be, it can be helpful to ask about the perceptions, concerns, and expectations of the people in "the system" (see *An anti-panic mindset* and the comments on a systemic approach).

Once you have a picture of an interconnected system, asking about perceptions, concerns, and expectations for the channels connecting the system members opens up many possibilities. For example:

- "What do you think/worries you about/are you expecting from X?"
- "How do you think Y views the situation at Z?"; "Do you know what concerns Y may have about Z?"; "What does Y expect from X?"
- "What is your general perception of our company?"; "Do you have particular concerns about us?"; "What are you hoping we can do for you?"

Solicitations

Solicitations to do something must always be clear and precise. Remember: feelings are running high. We do not want to further inflate the troll with an exchange such as this one:

"Could you open the file so that we can look at it together?" (gritting teeth)

"Which file?" (mirroring the other person's stress)

"The one from yesterday." (impatience growing)

"The Word doc or the Excel?"

"The PowerPoint!" (becoming quite annoyed)

"There wasn't any. The only PowerPoint was sent on Tuesday!"

"Okay then, the one from Tuesday!" (beginning to lose it)

"Right. Now, where is the $#%@& share screen button gone?"

When you read the above dialogue while sitting calmly, you may find it hard to criticize the opening solicitation, "Could you open the file ..." This is because, in normal circumstances, it would be perfectly acceptable. However, in a candid exchange, you must be unusually careful, and, in this case, perhaps the reference to "the file" should be more specific. Tempers are already frayed, so you must strive to avoid further misunderstanding.

And if it was impossible to be precise, you could have started by asking, for example, "Do you have a file we could look at together so we can be sure we're both referring to the same data?"

In a candid exchange, the safest type of solicitation is what's called a Connection Request[19]. For example:

- "Could you show me...?"
- "May I ask you to step outside with me for a minute...?"
- "Could we call X now and find out from them...?"

Notice that Connection Requests use the present tense and are in some way concerned with a relationship. Such a request, therefore, automatically moves you toward the issue at the heart of any difficult conversation—the misalignment of people's viewpoints and interests. While talking about facts, figures, objects, methods, history, and so on may seem more comfortable, a candid exchange is about relationships, and it is thus appropriate to use Connection Requests.

Of course, there is an overlap between invitations, inquiries, and solicitations. A solicitation can also be an invitation, for example, and all three of the Connection Request examples given above are invitations in the form of a solicitation. However, the invitation-enquiry-solicitation distinction is useful when meta-communicating about difficult conversations, as we are now, or when you analyze your discussions after they have occurred.

Listen

In some ways, listening is the opposite of explaining. Your challenge is to understand how the other party sees things (instead of explaining your viewpoint), empathize with them (instead of expressing your feelings), and gain insight into what they fundamentally need (instead of identifying and communicating your needs). Although you may not appear to be active on the surface, you are incredibly busy underneath, keeping your mind under control.

We should spend a lot of time listening. In some instances, especially when the other person is angry or irritated, 99% of your efforts are concentrated on listening, as almost anything you say will worsen matters. By allowing others to release their feelings, high-quality listening contributes significantly to the candid exchange's goal of achieving calm.

Listening carefully is also important for checking the optimistic pre-suppositions mentioned in the section *An anti-panic mindset*. It helps you notice any inconsistencies in what the other person is saying, allowing you to understand the nature of their intentions (Win-Win, Win-Lose, etc.), and alerting you to unacceptable prejudices.

In addition, attentive listening can tell you whether the other person considers you to be in or out of their crowd. When you have a positive predisposition toward someone, you tend to assume that they will feel the same way toward you—but this can be a mistake.

For example, you could assume that, since you are on the same team, the other person thinks you are okay, although they do not see it that way. Maybe they see themselves as a "worker" and you as a "manager," and since you do not "get your hands dirty," you're out! Or maybe they see themselves as young and cool, and you are past your sell-by date—out again!

For all these reasons, you should listen for your own good—and not just because you are nice. To do so, you need to *accept whatever situation you find yourself in* so that your mind is ready to listen—not wandering off with thoughts of the way things should be or should have been. Then *listen*, of course, though we will see that this is not as simple as it may sound. Finally, *keep an open mind* about what you hear. This will maximize the effectiveness of your listening.

~~Listen to confirm a viewpoint~~

~~Ideate or dream~~

~~Contemplate my next move~~

Accept the situation

It's water under the bridge. What's past has passed. Don't look back. Let bygones be bygones. No use crying over spilled milk. Carpe diem.

These well-known slogans make sense, of course, but they are easier said than done. Although you might be familiar with them, when the conversation goes off the rails, your mind gets occupied with thoughts of disapproval, disgust, disappointment, loss, and so on. And you cannot listen. For one thing, your self-talk is justifying your past actions. This prevents you from seeing ways out of your predicament, since you are still in denial of the present situation.

The power of abandoning the past

A friend of mine is a real estate lawyer. She mainly works with the top people in large companies and on new developments—she was involved in the redevelopment of the King's Cross area in London, for example.

One day, she was asked to act as an intermediary in resolving several long-running disputes. Her colleagues had a hunch that she might succeed where they'd been stuck.

Indeed, that's what happened. When my friend told me about this, she laughed. "It was so easy!" she said. "All I had to do was stop people talking about the past. Once they'd understood that I refused to go over old ground and judge right and wrong, the progress was amazing!"

Imagine some of your past disputes and how they might have been if everyone had let bygones be bygones to focus on what to do going forward!

Of course, a certain knowledge of past events can help you understand the present situation, but it is crucial not to judge those events or the people involved in them, as this will pollute your listening. The issue of who's right and who's wrong is both emotive and subjective. It's impossible to decide, so why use mental energy trying? It is better to accept the current situation and use that energy to focus on the other party and what they are saying.

Accepting for the moment

The above arguments notwithstanding, acceptance can be extremely hard to achieve. Consider, for example, the following situations:

- Your boss tells you that, following failures to deliver and complaints from your team, he's demoting you. You're no longer the team leader.
- Your doctor informs you that you're paralyzed from the waist down and that you'll need drugs and physiotherapy for the rest of your life.
- Your stock broker explains that the structured investment you trusted with nearly all your capital has failed and that your other shares are also down. You're ruined.

In these circumstances, your attention might seem riveted on your boss, doctor, or stockbroker, but your listening may be deficient. You probably had an idea of what the other party would tell you before the conversation began. Still, it is equally likely that you have already started to deny what's happened, and you just can't believe it when your boss, doctor, or stockbroker describes your predicament! Instead, you spend a lot of mental energy trying to make what you hear fit with your theories.

As they speak, your mind darts off in multiple directions, trying to understand what's being said and linking the ideas to what you already know. You are distracted, and even if you manage to ask a few questions, you'll look back on the conversation later and lament things you should have asked but didn't.

The consequences of what you're hearing are also in your mind. What if this and that? How can you get them to ...? Will you be able to ...? Your thoughts leap toward your future situation.

In circumstances like these, fully accepting the current situation in the short time available would be a superhuman achievement—fortunately, it's unnecessary.

With a little mental agility, you can say to yourself, "*For the moment*, I'll accept that ..."

For example, "For the moment, I'll accept that I've completely botched this team leader job," or, "For the moment, I'll accept that I won't walk again," or, "For the moment, I'll accept that I'm ruined."

Somehow, the simple phrase "for the moment" allows you to temporarily enter a reality you'd prefer not to see. To do this, you can use a trick you are already very good at, having practiced it thousands of times when watching TV and films: you suspend disbelief.

In this case, unlike when watching a film, it's the *real* world that you disbelieve, denying things that you can't yet cope with or which contradict your interests, values and beliefs.

Using suspension of disbelief, you can put aside one set of beliefs and try out another. For instance, you can say to yourself, "Let's suppose that what the client says is true..." and then act upon that working assumption. Maybe things will work out better that way.

The positive initial assumptions for a candid exchange, described in the chapter *Candid and Calming Communication*, are also good examples of how temporarily adopting a useful belief can benefit the outcome of a discussion.

In summary, while having a difficult conversation, it's much easier and more practical to accept a situation *for the moment* rather than trying to fully accept an unpleasant reality in a few seconds. When you do this, you no longer need to ignore or twist facts that don't fit your current point of view, so you put yourself in a better position to hear and learn from whatever the other party is saying.

Just listen

Just listening means concentrating on what is said rather than ideating or dreaming.

When listening to another person, you hear N voices, N-1 of which are inside your head. These N-1 voices are your internal dialogue, an extremely real conversation between the different functional  parts of your brain. Stimulated by what you're hearing, your creative part is coming up with all sorts of ideas. Other parts assess these ideas, taking up valuable brain power and having a noisy discussion. A further part is way off track, worrying about an issue that has been on your mind for days.

The challenge of "just listening" has thus two main aspects: quieting internal voices and paying attention to external ones. It can be further enhanced by Threefold Listening, which I discuss in a moment.

Quieting internal voices

The apparent remedy for this internal chatter is to tell it to shut up, but that approach can backfire. It simply adds another stressed inner voice shouting, "Shut up!" It's better to accept that your mind is a busy and noisy place and, whenever you get distracted, drag it back to focus on the other party (this is the approach taken in meditation, which is why this practice can strengthen listening skills).

As mentioned, the voice you're supposed to be listening to—that of the other party—is also a source of distraction, since it stimulates multiple lines of thought. They are often triggered when the other party describes a problem. A possible solution comes to mind, and you begin to think about this instead of paying attention to what's being said. Once again, the best solution is acknowledging the distraction without getting upset and returning your focus to listening.

When listening (as for asking), it's best to concentrate on the present. You must be aware of your mind running off into the past or the future. Thoughts involving the past are usually about understanding or justifying the current situation. It's often necessary to do this, but not while you're supposed to be listening.

As for the future, I have already mentioned the danger of thinking about solutions. Another common error is thinking about what to say next while waiting to reply. Perhaps you detect a criticism while listening, for example, so you start planning, word by word, how to counter it. Composing your masterpiece reply takes up most of your attention, leaving little for listening.

This habit of planning your next move is both *unnecessary* and *damaging*. It is unnecessary because if you have the presence and patience to pause after listening, this pause will allow you to compose your reply. It is damaging because it reduces your effectiveness as a listener and may give the impression that you are not listening—it's a significant risk since, of course, you are not!

Ironically, the speed of your response to what the other person is saying gives you away. It is evident that you are listening if you pause before giving a thoughtful reply. However, when, a microsecond after the other person stops talking, you respond with a self-serving comment or question, then it's evident that you haven't heard a word of what they just told you!

Paying attention

What do you concentrate on if you're hurtling downhill, over rocks and tree roots, on a cross-country bike? The price you paid for the mountain lift? The café that you will visit at the bottom of the run? Or the rocks and the roots?

It's apparent that you should concentrate on what's happening in front of you in the present. What's more difficult is to do the same when you're in front of someone who's saying things you don't want to hear, and the past and future are crammed with causes for concern. So, you must concentrate on paying attention!

In addition to being mindful, as we'll discuss below, I suggest two simple measures to make listening more effective.

The first is to *banish potential distractions* wherever possible. Mindful listening is no easy business, so why let distractions make it even more complicated?

At a meeting on foreign territory—in someone's office or home, for example—you can at least turn off your phone. Where you control your surroundings, you can clear the desk, turn computers and screens off, and perhaps remove the biscuit tin. On a video call, you close superfluous windows and disable desktop notifications. A neutral background might also be better than a tropical paradise or a scene from a space movie.

A second, slightly paradoxical measure is to *interrupt in the service of listening*.

The guideline "Just listen" should not be interpreted as meaning "Never interrupt." It's fine to interrupt when you've lost track of what the speaker is saying, when you feel yourself about to lose concentration, or when you can see that the speaker needs encouragement[20]. To do so, you may use a question or attempt to reformulate what the other person has said, for example.

Listening in conversation is not the same as listening to the radio. The latter doesn't involve any cooperation between the transmitter and receiver, whereas an exchange cannot happen without interactions between the protagonists.

Remember, however, that although you may interrupt to facilitate the candid exchange, you must not do so to "make it about you." That is, it's *not* okay to interrupt to show how clever you are or to recount an anecdote that has just come to mind. Someone striving to communicate their problems and needs doesn't want to hear your war stories!

> ***Even the best listeners get distracted***
>
> *Everyone interprets, evaluates, and ideates when they should be listening. It's natural! The trick is to recognize these distractions and put them aside as quickly as possible.*
>
> *Taking notes may help—scribbling a few words that capture a distracting idea allows you to concentrate on the other person again, for example.*
>
> *You may also ask for assistance: "I'm sorry, I got distracted for a second. Could you repeat that?" This mini-interruption is a genuine sign that you are trying to listen.*
>
> *Remember that it is perfectly natural to get distracted. Do not worry about it. Just try to reduce the time lost while you restore your concentration*

Threefold listening

To harvest as much information as possible from an exchange, Vincent Lenhardt, a leader in the coaching profession, suggests that you *listen threefold* (Lenhardt):

1. To what the other person says
2. To their secondary signals, such as voice, tone, and body language
3. To your own reactions.

While the first two types of listening are often discussed, much less is said of the third, which requires that you pay attention to *your reactions* to what is being said and use these reactions as a source of information.

As you listen to the other party, ideas and images emerge, and emotions stir. If you can use them to better understand what you are hearing, then you are engaged in type three listening.

For example, you might feel excitement, disgust, or fear as you listen to a colleague. When this happens, you first ask yourself, "Is this feeling mine?" Your colleague could be the source of emotions that you detect through a kind of resonance. Just as two weights suspended from a single wire will oscillate in harmony, and if you start swinging one of them, then the other will follow, so two communicating individuals transfer emotions between them. When someone is explaining something to you and is excited, you become excited. If they're disgusted by something, this disgust is passed on to you. If they're afraid, you start to feel nervous, and so on.

Suppose you decide that the feeling in question—say, it's nervousness—is coming from your colleague, you can use this information. For example, you could note "nervousness!" Alternatively, you might draw their attention to the nervousness and ask about it: "It seems to me that you're worried about this. Why are you so concerned?" Depending on the circumstances and the sensed feeling, you can play out the scene however you like.

Of course, it's also possible that what you're feeling is homegrown. That is, the sensed feeling is not being *transmitted* by another person, though it is probably *triggered* by them. For example, a colleague might suggest working with someone whom you know from a previous disagreeable experience, and unpleasant emotional memories rise up when you consider this possibility. In this case, you conclude that what you feel belongs to you and is linked to the story you're telling yourself about the person in question.

When you notice self-generated emotions such as the one just described, it's a warning sign. To avoid falling into the trap of emotional reasoning, you must acknowledge this signal but avoid responding emotionally. You can choose to do this by making a shorthand note to yourself. For example: "Heck. N mentioned Jan. Problem!" This is a trick I recommend for dealing with transmitted emotions, and it works similarly. By recording the emotion, you distance yourself from it, observing but not being led by it.

Another possibility is to share your feelings with the other party to get them out into the open. "Alex, I have had dealings with Jan in the past, and we fell out quite badly. Just hearing the name gets me upset. I want to let you know, as it's obviously relevant." Such a statement may avoid later misunderstandings and is consistent with our candid exchange objective of calm dialogue.

However you decide to deal with the rising emotions, whether they are received from others or internally generated, it's better to be aware of them. Type three listening gives you this awareness.

Remain open-minded

Keeping an open mind means listening to understand instead of listening to respond.

It's not so much a thing to do as an attitude to adopt. There are fewer barriers when your mind is open to new information and ideas. The other person's message no longer has to fight past the mental obstacles you place in its path. You suspend judgment, and you delay any interpretation until the other party stops talking.

Suspending judgment

Open-mindedness is receptiveness to new ideas, and to achieve this state, you have to suspend judgment. This requires a particular mental effort because you are required to hold multiple, perhaps contradictory, thoughts simultaneously. Listening is easier if you can put things in convenient mental boxes as soon as you hear them, but if you're open-minded, you can't just label things as good or bad, cheap or expensive, and so on.

Open-mindedness is not tolerance. Madeline Albright[21] clarified the difference between these two concepts as follows: "I don't like the word 'tolerance' because that means to tolerate, to put up with. It's more important to respect."

Respecting another point of view is challenging when what you hear contradicts your opinions, values, and beliefs. It is also hard when you have something at stake.

Suppose, for example, that a friend borrows your car for the evening and brings it back with a huge, expensive-looking dent. When such an incident occurs, the troll is very likely to appear.

Noticing him at the door, trying to get into the room, it is crucial that you fight the temptation to think in terms of good/bad, right/wrong, and so on. All the measures being discussed here, which allow you to hear the whole account right to the end before analyzing it, will help.

Everyday life will throw many challenges at your attempts to suspend judgment. You must become an expert troll detector and recognize the circumstances where it is hard to achieve open-mindedness. When you can, you will be better able to tackle each challenge.

Note-taking

Suppose a customer (internal or external) is explaining their issues with a report you've written. They say, "... and I'm afraid that the cost analysis section isn't clear enough ...." It's a difficult conversation because you've worked hard on the report, you're proud of it, and you find criticism hard to take. At the same time, the client urgently needs to understand specific information, and they've been requesting a clarification for some time. The atmosphere is tense.

If you genuinely attempt to understand your customer's problem—to see why the report isn't clear enough *to them*—then they will probably feel reassured and cooperate with you, allowing you to fix the issues together.

However, if you tell yourself, for example, "They're stupid," or, "You can't expect a report like this to be clear the first time—you've got to work through the figures," or "They think writing this sort of thing is easy!", then you start a negative train of thought. Following this train, you justify your position to yourself, reinforce self-limiting beliefs, bolster your low opinion of those around you, and cease to listen with an open mind.

With such a challenge, and once again, note-taking can be a great help. By concentrating on capturing critical conversation points on paper, you delay interpreting what you're hearing and seeing. Note-taking also helps your memory and allows you to quote the other person verbatim, if necessary, using their vocabulary. Accurate recall and playback of what is said demonstrate that you are listening and help avoid misunderstandings due to misinterpreted words. Above all, note-taking helps you relax and listen more open-mindedly, since it removes the pressure of processing what you're hearing before you forget it.

Notes are just one solution to the challenge of capturing what someone is saying rather than a distorted version of it. People use many other tricks (Google "active listening" for ideas!), and I leave you to work out what's best for you.

Benefits of open-mindedness

Research shows that open-mindedness could be worth the effort. According to the Positive Psychology Center at the University of Pennsylvania (Seligman), open-minded people

- are more resistant to suggestion and manipulation;
- are less likely to project their feelings and viewpoints onto others;
- tend to score better on tests of general cognitive ability.

However, we don't know the direction of the cause and effect—in my opinion, research will show that the dependency is circular.

The first two points on this list essentially say that open-mindedness makes us more resilient to thinking errors that make us susceptible to manipulation and assuming that others think as we do. As Kahneman explains in his seminal book *Thinking Fast and Slow*, manipulation techniques exploit fast, instinctive survival reflexes. In other words, they take advantage of easy rather than effortful thinking. Similarly, projecting your thoughts on others—assuming that they think as we do—is easier than being open-minded toward others. Therefore, it seems likely that open-mindedness, which requires more effort than instinctive reaction, counteracts some of the thinking errors we discussed. It keeps us thinking straight in trying circumstances.

There is also evidence that time pressure and fatigue degrade open-mindedness. For example, one study[22] analyzed over a thousand parole hearings conducted by senior judges. Every day, each judge decided on each of the 14 to 35 cases that came before them, spending an average of some 6 minutes per decision, and the research shows that the cognitive availability of judges had a significant effect on the likelihood of prisoners being released or not. At the beginning of the day or after a break, the judge was more lenient than at the end of the day or after a long series of decisions. The more tired they were, the more likely it was that the judges' brains would opt for the least effortful choice: denial of parole.

Hence, cultivating open-mindedness is a case of understanding and fighting back your favorite thinking errors, especially when you're tired or stressed.

There is, of course, a strong link between open-mindedness and mindfulness. Shunryu Suzuki's seminal book on meditation and practice, *Zen Mind, Beginner's Mind* (Suzuki), begins thus: "If your mind is empty, it is always ready for anything; it is open to everything. In the beginner's mind there are many possibilities, but in the expert's there are few."

Quality listening requires mindfulness

Accepting the situation, just listening, and remaining open-minded all revolve around mindfulness, a fundamental component of quality listening. Indeed, *mindful listening* may be considered a more advanced practice than active listening, which relies more on remembering *what to do* when listening than on *how to be*.

For example, Googling "active listening" quickly unearths advice such as the following:

- Keep eye contact.
- Don't think about your next question.
- Reformulate what the other person says.
- Pay attention to your body language.
- Take notes.

While I agree that all these behaviors are desirable, many *result from* quality listening—they don't produce it. For example, eye contact with another person happens automatically when you are listening. Also, your body language shows that you're listening—you don't need to make any special effort. Since you will concentrate on what's being said, you won't be thinking about the next question. You will feel the need to reformulate if it's necessary or if you see that the other party is worried that you haven't understood.

Mindfulness, however, is not a behavior but a quality of being. Just as you can say that you are being thoughtful or careful, so you can say that you're being mindful. The ability to remain mindful while working, playing, and under stress can be achieved with training and requires regular practice. Jon Kabat-Zinn[23] defines mindfulness as "Paying attention in a particular way, on purpose, in the present moment, and nonjudgmental", which demonstrates its relevance to listening (Kabat-Zinn).

Rebecca Shafir[24] asserts that mindful listening helps you pay attention for longer and retain more information (Shafir). She also likens it to stroking a pet. By moving your focus away from yourself and to the other person, you distance yourself from your anxieties. Your blood pressure drops, and you feel calmer. The other person not only picks up on this and mirrors your calmness but also feels the release of tension from being closely listened to.

Most mindfulness gurus are humble enough to admit that they don't have a formula for being mindful. They point out that mindfulness is a personal thing, and everyone has to find their way. Even so, certain basic practices, such as meditation, help most people.

Given that there are no universal rules for mindfulness, I will limit this commentary to a few things I've discovered during my practice. Though not original, they may be helpful to you, and they are also directly relevant to mindful listening.

I have gradually reduced the rules I follow to two short phrases, and I use them to get back to a mindful state when my concentration dwindles:

- Let it go.
- Bring it back.

Through mindfulness training, you can become more aware of your distractions and get better at handling them. Hence, "Let it go" refers to the images and ideas that pop into your mind and disrupt your concentration; it is a reminder to not hold on to them, not to explore them or think about them, but to let them drift away of their own accord.

"Bring it back" is a reminder to return to your chosen subject of focus.

I have learned to accept that my mind will often wander from the chosen subject of focus, such as my breath. Furthermore, I now realize that distraction is an important part of mindfulness practice and should be welcomed as such.

It is impossible to practice without distractions. Without them, you would not have to make any effort, and you would not improve. Mindfulness practice without distractions would be akin to weight training without any weights!

In fact, weight training, exercise, and sports offer excellent opportunities to practice mindfulness—meditation is not the only way.

To make mindfulness practice part of your routine, it helps to think of it as a kind of mind supervision: you are strengthening your ability to engage the different parts of your mind as and when you want them to work instead of being a slave to obsessions and wandering thoughts.

When practicing mindfulness (as opposed to using mindfulness in an operational context), you tell your mind to ignore mental distractions and concentrate on observing your body's autonomic actions.

In classical meditation practice, the breath is the subject of focus, as it is controlled by the autonomic nervous system, which means that you can observe it without having to will it to operate. However, the body is capable of doing other things automatically, such as walking, running, cycling, and repeated lifting. Therefore, you can practice mindfulness when you walk your dog, when you are on your exercise bike, and so on, changing the subject of your focus accordingly (to the feeling of your feet hitting the ground, to the sensation of the pedals turning, and so on).

When listening, you are *being* mindful, rather than training to be mindful. This is when you use the fruits of your practice. In a listening context, "Bring it back" reminds you to focus on the speaker. Thanks to mindfulness training, you will be able to better return your focus on the speaker without feeling guilty about getting distracted—you will get used to and accept the fact that your mind will wander off occasionally.

These comments notwithstanding, I would like to stress that mindful listening is effortful. It is based on mindfulness, which is a discipline in itself. However, it is an effective discipline, as Gandhi reminded us when he said, "I have so much to accomplish today that I must meditate for two hours instead of one."

Explain

It is tempting to think that being anxious about a difficult conversation can be overcome by carefully preparing an explanation of the facts of the current situation (the external world), how you feel about that situation (your internal world), and what you want. However, the diagram below highlights two shortcomings of this idea.

First, you can rarely restrict yourself to facts. Your assessment of those facts will slip into your description of the situation, and rightly so. Unless you explain your assessment, the other party is unlikely to understand your point of view.

Second, the conversational dynamic may change how you feel and the outcome you desire. As new information becomes available through discussion, you predict alternative future situations. You assess these possibilities, and your internal world reacts in some way—you feel something new. As a result, you may discover that what you thought you needed must be reviewed.

By all means, be well-prepared for your difficult conversations, but be careful not to develop a static point of view[25]. A candid exchange is a dynamic process, which means that explanations cannot be rehearsed and perfected in advance.

However, you can decide in advance to communicate in a way that ensures your explanations are accepted. This can be done without diluting what you want to say. To achieve this at any moment in an exchange —whether you are explaining facts, feelings, or needs—ask yourself the following question:

- "How can I explain my understanding as accurately as possible?"

This simple question is a powerful antidote to the complexity of a candid exchange. Of course, its effectiveness depends on you adopting the CCC mindset. Assuming that you do, the intention to explain just an *understanding* substantially reduces the chance of an adverse reaction. In fact, quite the opposite could happen: the other party may spontaneously respond by sharing their understanding.

In the following sections[26], you will see how this approach works when sharing observations, revealing feelings, and describing needs[27].

Share observations

Let's distinguish between first-order, factual observations and second-order observations resulting from your assessment. Factual observations are based solely on directly perceived information (what you see, read, hear, etc.), whereas assessments are the result of your interpretations, evaluations, and predictions.

The "share observations" guideline encourages you to explain the information you receive from both these sources. However, it is often a good idea to start explanations with purely factual observations. This avoids the tricky business of sharing an assessment, and it is also easier than revealing feelings or describing needs.

Another reason to start with facts is that a quick fact check may allow you to fix any error in your observations, thereby avoiding unnecessary bad feelings. If you were to state that the software product being discussed costs $500, and your colleague believes it costs 500 €, this can easily be checked by visiting a website, for example.

While making assessment-based observations, you must be careful to avoid tyrannical assessments, which I discussed in the chapter *Candid and Calming Communication*. Otherwise, you'd be implicitly sharing your opinions and other subjective matter along with objective data. As explained earlier, assessments comprise interpretations, evaluations, and predictions, and they become tyrannical when concealed.

Let's see how this plays out with a couple of sketches.

The late code release

Consider the situation of a team of software developers discussing their upcoming code release:

- Someone kicks things off with, "I looked at last night's regression results, and we're late!" A junior member of the team is clearly irritated by this remark but says nothing.
- Someone else then chips in: "If the release isn't made this week, the customer's going to be upset." Then someone else objects: "No. Fred's cool if she gets the release by next Wednesday. She won't be bothered at all."
- Another team member complains, "But it's crucial to make the release this week!" then a colleague bristles, "Not at all. Finishing the user interface is much more important!"
- One more voice is heard: "We told the customer that we would deliver this week, and the customer is king. We must make the release by Friday." This doesn't go down well with someone else, who objects: "Who says so? It's a public holiday on Thursday, and I deserve a break. The management should be more careful with its planning!"

Although the subject under discussion is, on the surface, purely technical, and you would expect a group of engineers to be able to deal with such issues in a cool, rational way, a difficult conversation has evidently developed. The way each person has presented their assessment of the situation seems to be an important contributing factor, so let's look at the interpretations, evaluations, and predictions made by the different protagonists.

Consider the opening remark: "..., and we're late!" This is an *evaluation*, although it is expressed as though it were indisputably true. Hence, it is a tyrannical interpretation (see *Assessment tyranny* and tyrannical assessments).

If the statement appears innocuous to you, that's probably because this way of talking is concise, convenient, and culturally acceptable. However, when a troll makes his presence felt in a conversation, it can trigger resistance and even conflict. Notice that, in the sketch, a junior member of the team becomes annoyed when they hear the remark.

Instead of "...we're late!" it would have been less provocative to say, for example, "... I think we're late," or, better still, "..., based on my calculations, we are a week behind schedule." These alternatives clarify that the speaker is making a deduction based on the data they've gathered rather than, for example, making a thinly disguised complaint about the rate of progress or a criticism of the people responsible for the delay.

The second alternative, while longer, is clearly the less controversial since the interpretation is more concrete: "We are a week behind schedule," rather than "We're late!"

The next exchange starts with "..., the customer's going to be upset," which is a *tyrannical prediction* and also includes mindreading (the projection about the customer's state of mind). Unsurprisingly, this comment is received with resistance, and the pushback is also in the form of an unqualified and tyrannical comment: "No. Fred's cool if ...." The atmosphere is becoming combative.

Then another team member complains: "But it's crucial to make the release this week!" This leads to another retort: "Not at all. Finishing the user interface is much more important!"

"It's crucial..." and "...is much more important!" are *judgments*. Both phrases are *evaluations*, but grammatically speaking, they are expressed as facts. They are, therefore, tyrannical and have the power to provoke defensiveness, resistance, aggression, etc.

Note that *qualified* evaluations would be okay. For example, the person who said, "It's crucial to make the release this week" might have been better advised to say, "It's *important to me* that we make the release this week." The latter sentence is more accurate than the original. It reveals how the person feels, and in contrast to the case where a judgment was pronounced, the rest of the team will probably treat such feelings with respect. For example, someone might respond, "Okay, I hear you, but the user interface is more important to me." We now have the ingredients for a debate rather than an argument.

Similarly, the phrase containing "... the customer is king..." is a tyrannical evaluation and might have been better expressed as follows:

"For me, the customer is king, and so I would be disappointed if we didn't make the release this week."

In all the above cases, the alternative, non-tyrannical formulations are more verbose and less intuitive than the original, and this tends to be so when you make an effort to share an assessment while reducing the risk of being misunderstood.

There is at least one more evaluation in the sketch—a rule that I have not commented on. See if you can find it!

The smelly cubicle cohabitant

The following sketch illustrates a situation that demands delicate handling.

Let's say you have a colleague with whom you share a small office. This colleague cycles to work, and you are talking to them about it, its uphill aspect, its perspirational consequences, and the resulting odor. In other words, you're trying to tell them that they smell.

Suppose you say, "Nicky, you're probably not aware of this, and I'm sure you can't help it after all the cycling uphill and stuff, but there's a funny and sweaty smell hanging around here. As you know, with clients visiting and all, we've got to be careful that …."

These words seem reasonable to you, and you don't see how Nicky could object to them. However, this is probably because you've been thinking about what to say for days.

Unfortunately, this preparation has backfired. By agonizing about your smelly cubicle and rehearsing what you're going to say, you ended up being unnecessarily verbose.

Moreover, you've provided several triggers for an argument:

- "You're probably not aware of this" is a thought projection.
- "Funny and sweaty smell" contains a judgment.
- "We've got to be careful that …" is a rule.

If Nicky is in a bad mood or feeling particularly sensitive that day, they might respond with any of the following lines:

- "Are you calling me stupid? Of course, I'm aware of it …."
- "What do you mean "funny"? It's just normal, clean sweat! If you got off your butt occasionally, you might know more about it …."
- "Don't you tell me about how to look after visitors! I've been doing this job for 20 years and …."

This illustrates that, by overthinking what you wanted to say to Nicky, you ended up with a little speech that was not as neutral as you had intended. You need to be extremely careful with your tyrannical assessments! Phrases such as "Are you aware that …," "I'm disturbed by a smell in this office," and "I believe we should be careful …" might have been easier for Nicky to hear.

Perhaps you could start with the following: "Nicky, you've been cycling to work now for about six weeks, right?" You could then allow them to respond—you're not delivering a prepared speech but simply initiating a discussion.

Nicky can then confirm or correct your data (perhaps it's seven weeks?). They could even guess where you are going with this. They themselves might have started to wonder about their sweat glands already, so it's possible that their response would be something like, "You're going to tell me that I smell, right?" At this point, the candid exchange is over, and we're back to a normal conversation. Job done!

However, if they simply confirm your observation, you need to go further. "Well, I notice you've been sweating on the days you cycle. Have you noticed this yourself?"

Again, you stay factual and concise. It's crucial not to go too far without giving the other person a chance to react. If you listen and watch, their reactions will guide what you should say next. Once again, the hard work could even be over if the message becomes clear to Nicky.

However, if Nicky simply replies with a "No," you must continue. "OK, I can understand how you could miss this. On the other hand, three of our colleagues commented that our box smelled sweaty last week. Given that I've noticed this, and others have too, what do you think?"

At this point, Nicky may acknowledge an issue, and you discuss what can be done (you'll be back to a regular discussion). If not, and assuming you don't have any fancy measuring equipment to help prove your case, then you have a decision to make. Do you consider that Nicky has not understood, or do you now believe that they are refusing to discuss the issue? In the first case, you will continue to carefully explain the problem that you perceive; perhaps, you could then talk about the difficulties this situation is causing you, or you might decide to stop here.

It's important to remember that you can abort this conversation. It is not always possible to reconcile differing points of view with a candid exchange, and you must recognize when your best efforts have failed. If you don't, then the likely consequences are as follows:

- You become progressively more frustrated, both with yourself and the other person, making the situation worse and increasing the chances of damaging the relationship.
- You miss the opportunity to take alternative and timely action.

"Alternative and timely action" is a way of saying controlled fight, flight, or freeze. In a professional context, a controlled fight often means escalating an issue to management, and controlled flight means withdrawal—avoiding or working around a problem rather than solving it. In this example, you could perhaps move to another office. A controlled freeze would mean agreeing with the other party to postpone the candid exchange to another time.

Notice that these examples, these frozen texts on a page, can give you the impression that there is only one correct outcome for each of the cases I presented—nothing could be further from the truth. Difficult conversations are, at best, complex; at worst, chaotic. You must hang on tight, responding as best you can to whatever comes up.

Reveal feelings

Imagine the following difficult conversations:

- You've messed up your calendar and must explain to your partner that, instead of going out with them this evening, you must work late.
- You've messed up your roadmap and must explain to your boss that, instead of being able to supply a vaccine just in time to save the world from a pandemic, you have to go back to the drawing board while your competitors make a fortune.

In both the above cases, we can imagine emotions raging—there's a giant troll to tame!

So, what do you say to your partner or boss to help them stay calm? What do you say to *yourself* to manage your emotions?

Furthermore, should you talk about feelings? I suggest that there is little choice.

Feelings insist on being heard

If you ignore the hurt, the rage, or the fear of the person you're talking to, they will invariably keep signaling these feelings until you acknowledge them somehow. They may look more miserable, speak louder, or just leave the room or cut the call.

The same goes for your internal self. Several psychological models use the idea of multiple voices within a person, and your internal dialogue is a conversation between these voices. If the voice that's crying "I am hurt!" or "I'm mad!" or "Get me out of here!" is ignored, then it will keep screaming so loudly that you will not be able to think.

Hence, the troll represents two sets of emotional commotion—your own and that of the other party—and both insist on being heard. Happily, if you do a good job of expressing your emotions, it usually makes the other party more inclined to explain theirs. Therefore, although accurately expressing emotions is not easy, you'll find it to be incredibly powerful when you get used to doing it.

There are two main aspects to this: accessing and identifying your emotions and expressing them accurately to avoid common pitfalls.

Accessing your emotions

As mentioned earlier when discussing the Pause, the story you tell yourself determines your emotional state—the more accurately you tell this story, the calmer you will tend to be. Furthermore, accessing your internal dialogue gives you information about your feelings—this is vital if you want to express them accurately.

For example, suppose you get CC'ed on an email to your boss (N+1) from your team member (N-1). It contains a suggestion for something that is your direct responsibility, and your immediate reactions might be as follows:

- What a lack of respect! (a judgment)
- A team member should never communicate with their N+2 without first contacting their team leader (a rule)
- They did this because they wanted to look good! (a projection and an assumption)

Pause. You are getting upset, so you must examine your internal dialogue.

The three bullet points above summarize the story you're telling yourself. When you become aware of this, you realize that you feel offended by the apparently disrespectful behavior, and you're angry. You also feel let down by your team member, whom you had considered a loyal rising star.

Notice that accessing your internal dialogue facilitates articulating confusing emotions. A feeling is a mix of emotions, and identifying individual ones is as hard as picking out all the ingredients in a ratatouille or the instruments in a large orchestra. However, different emotions are associated with each thread of the story you're telling yourself, and so accessing your internal dialogue helps unravel things.

You may also see the tyrannical assessment for what it is, leading you to question it. Perhaps you should check the details of what happened before getting any more upset. Therefore, you decide to call your team member and find out why they sent the mail (adopting an intention to understand). You ask, "I just received a copy of your email to X. What was the reason for it?" (factual observation + invitation).

It turns out that they had bumped into your boss, who'd asked them to send this mail without delay. They had called you twice, got no reply, waited a bit, and then CC'ed you and sent it.

While you still disagree with their decision to send the mail, you've completely rewritten the story you are telling yourself. You are now calm and engaged in a normal conversation with your team member.

This example also illustrates the point I made earlier about the dynamic nature of a difficult conversation—as it proceeds, new information comes to light and is assessed with new self-talk. As your internal dialogue changes, so do your feelings. In this case, you might end up with, for instance, feelings of relief mixed with slight frustration.

Expressing feelings accurately

Over the years, certain types of tyrannical assessments have become instinctive—they kick in immediately after something happens or is said. You conceal them because they have become invisible to you, and you do this both when you talk out loud and in your internal dialogue.

Making and transmitting observations and identifying, managing, and expressing feelings are intricately connected topics. You observe and relate facts about a situation. This observation affects your feelings and those of others. You notice these feelings and may comment on them, and this, in turn, affects the general emotional situation.

To cope with these complex interactions, when expressing emotions, it helps to watch out for three sources of inaccuracy:

- *Accusations:* Statements about your feelings that attribute responsibility for them to someone or something else (attribution errors).
- *Confusions:* Expressions that have the form of feeling statements but are not really about feelings at all.
- *Substitutions:* Statements about emotions and feelings that are inaccurate because of wrong labeling.

When you make an *accusation*, you're trying to express genuine feelings, but perhaps because you deny or misunderstand their cause, you inadvertently transform your statement into an allegation.

For example, when you say, "You made me sad," you really mean, "Having thought about what you said, I am sad." Note that the latter statement is undeniable. You are the only person with direct access to your thoughts and emotions, so when you use the first-person singular to say what's happening inside you, others can't reasonably argue.

On the other hand, "You made me sad" is an accusation! Consider a few other accusations that we find in casual speech:

- "It makes me furious!"
- "They disgust me!"
- "He's driving me mad!"
- "This reorganization is stressing me out!"
- "They scare me to death!"
- "You're annoying me!"
- "It makes me depressed!"
- "This software is driving me up the wall!"

The common factor in these examples is that the speaker transfers responsibility for their feelings to someone or something else. They are saying that X caused a particular set of emotions within them, though, as we have seen, the real cause is the story they tell themselves about X. The above statements are thus *inaccurate* and may fuel an argument.

To avoid this pitfall, a simple and mighty weapon is available: the first-person singular: "I." When you say, "I am furious," "I feel disgust," "I feel like I'm going mad," and so on, you move away from accusations and, instead, describe the state you find yourself in. As already mentioned, you are the only person with access to this information, and these first-person statements are, therefore, less inflammatory.

Unlike concealed accusations, *feeling confusions* are not feelings but something else—a need, a request, an observation, or an opinion, for example.

When someone expresses an opinion as though it were a feeling, they are talking inaccurately. When they say, "I feel that you've made a mistake," for example, they could mean, "In my opinion, you've made a mistake," or perhaps, "You idiot, look at what you just did!" Either way, someone else making a mistake is not a feeling!

Here are a few other familiar confusions:

- "I feel it's your responsibility to <do X> ..." (request?)
- "I feel they don't like us..." (projection?)
- "I feel that's expensive..." (opinion?)
- "I feel that <X> is important..." (value?)
- "I'm sorry you did that..." (accusation?)
- "I'm afraid you'll have to..." (direction?)
- "I'm afraid I'll have to..." (an excuse for what they're about to do?)
- "I regret to tell you that..." ("I'm telling you!")

All the examples start with "feeling words," but they do not express emotions—at least, not clearly and directly. For this reason, these statements are inaccurate, even if "I" is used throughout.

To understand why this can be problematic, we invite you to replace each phrase with something less provocative. For example, instead of, "I feel it's your responsibility <do X>...", perhaps we could use, "I believe you are responsible for Y, so please could you <do X>?"

Finally, *feeling substitutions*, or rackets ("Racket Feeling"), are mislabeled feelings. In these, the person is affected by an emotion but is unable to identify it. For example, they say they are angry when they are afraid.

Feeling substitutions are emotional scars, often sustained early in life. For example, in Western culture, many people substitute fear with anger, as they have been brought up not to show fear. For similar reasons, others may hide anger and show sadness instead.

Given the deep-seated nature of racket emotions, there is no quick fix or formula for dealing with them. In practice, some people independently become conscious of their racket emotions and deliberately work to reduce their hold. Others get external help—a therapist, a coach, or a friend, perhaps.

In spite of the lack of an immediate solution for feeling substitutions, the concept enriches one's understanding of conversation dynamics. You realize that apparent emotions—yours and the other party's—don't always tell the whole story. When you detect anger, the authentic emotion may be fear. Similarly, a sad expression could result from a racket emotion rather than genuine sadness. Awareness of these possibilities can make you cautious about judging a situation too quickly.

Having represented this emotional cocktail as a troll, we now see that trolls, like people, are complicated.

Describe needs

Suppose a customer calls and says, "We've been trying to use the software you sold us and have run into difficulties. We missed a critical delivery last week, and management tells me that failure this week isn't an option. I'm very nervous and frustrated and fed up. I need to feel secure in my job and confident  in managing this project. I also want to have real partnerships with our suppliers. However, working with your support guys last week didn't work out well. Can you help?"

What can you say? You can see the pain they're in, you don't feel attacked, and you throw yourself into finding a solution for them. After all, they've given you all the ingredients—you understand what's happened, how they feel, and what they need.

Why might you feel committed to helping this customer? What have they said and *not* said?

This ideal customer exemplifies a crucial skill in difficult conversations: *expressing needs at a level that other parties can relate to.*

The described situation has all the ingredients for a difficult conversation: the customer is pressured, upset, and disappointed with your support. However, in spite of their uncomfortable feelings, they anticipated the troll and expressed themselves in a way that prevented him from turning up!

In a less ideal world, the customer might call your boss and threaten to bring the sky down if you don't send an expert to sort out their problem immediately, somewhere on site. Your boss would then call you; you would defend yourself and, then, extremely annoyed, start working out how to appease the &%**#$ customer.

In the above example, however, the customer starts factually and then responsibly expresses their feelings and needs. You find these needs easy to relate to since you, too, need job security, and when you have projects to manage, you also like to feel confident doing so. Since they are expressing their needs at a level you can relate to, you find yourself inclined to listen and help.

Furthermore, they explain several needs that are genuinely important to them—security, confidence, supplier relationships—and, finally, they leave you to make suggestions. Rather than demanding specific solutions, such as particular software fixes or special support, they let you respond as you see fit.

Levels

Needs can be organized in levels or layers, with fundamental needs at the bottom—security, connection, rest, etc.—and progressively more complex and specific needs higher up—physiotherapy, internet access, eating out, etc ("Maslow's Hierarchy of Needs").

Everyone has the same fundamental needs, but few people share the same high-level ones. For some, a transcendental experience may require travel to a far-away place, while others might prefer meditating quietly in their back garden.

Hence, when you express your needs at a lower, more fundamental level, it's more likely that the other party will understand and relate to them. For example, if you say that you are tired and need to take a break, most people will be able to relate to it. If, instead, you say that you need your software problems sorted out by the end of next week, then the other person is left to guess that your fundamental need is job security—that's asking a lot!

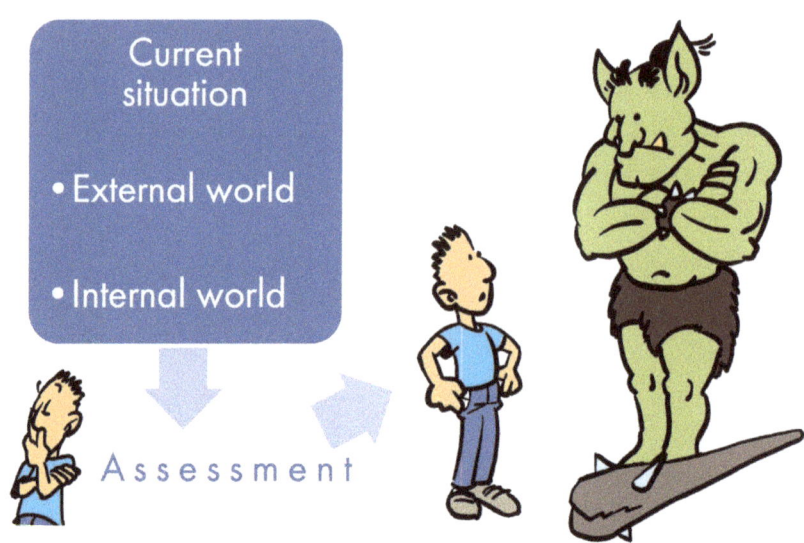

However, it's not always necessary to descend to the level of fundamental needs to be understood. It all depends on how much you have in common with the other party. If you say, "Boy, do I need a pizza" to a friend who understands that "pizza" also means stopping work and having a relaxing beer, then you don't need to spell out your fundamental need. They know you're not starving—this is not a physical security need!

Pizza talk aside, people often tend to express needs at a level others do not understand, obliging others to guess their motivation. Since the audience reacts to what is said rather than to the implied fundamental need, there is a good chance of misunderstanding. For example:

- "I want to quit this job" may stem from a more basic need, such as a new challenge or, quite different, a break.
- "I would like a salary increase" may be hiding something else— for instance, "I need to feel valued," or, perhaps, "I need to feel secure."

- "I want to leave [the party] now" may be motivated by the need for calm and rest or, on the contrary, to go somewhere more exciting.

To make needs still more difficult to understand, they are often expressed even more obscurely, almost violently. For example, the preceding examples could look like this:

- "I quit!"
- "I deserve a raise!"
- "Let's go!"
- "Clear up your room!"

You say these sorts of things out of habit and because it's quick and easy. However, as already mentioned in this chapter, it is wiser to express yourself more carefully during a candid exchange, even if this means using extra words.

With this in mind, let's look at Maslow's hierarchy of needs, starting at the highest level and working down, with examples of things that might satisfy needs at each level:

Self-actualization: Morality, creativity, spontaneity, acceptance, experience, and purpose. For example, completing a project you believe is of economic and/or social importance.

Self-esteem: Confidence, achievement, interdependence. For example, leading a team, helping your team members develop their autonomy.

Love and belonging: Friendship, family, intimacy, connection. For example, getting feedback from colleagues that shows you're considered "one of them."

Safety and security: Health, employment, property, family, and social ability. For example, being confident of keeping your job or, if not, of easily finding other ways to make a living.

Physiological needs: Air, food, water, shelter, clothing, and sleep. For example, the office heating and air conditioning systems work, and there is plenty of coffee.

At the lowest level, when talking about physiological needs, it actually makes sense to use the verb "need." For example, "I need to eat." Further up the hierarchy, verbs such as "want," "desire," and "like" may be more appropriate. For example, "I would like recognition for completing this work ahead of schedule" may be preferable to "I need recognition ...".

Being aware of these different levels not only helps structure your thinking but also hints at the danger of confusing, for example, operational requirements, ambitions, and desires with real needs.

Real needs

Since pinpointing your exact needs is a demanding business, a common mistake you might make is to start your sentence with, "I need ..." and follow it with something that is not a need at all!

For example:

- "I need clearer reports" is a *complaint*
- "I need you to move to another room" is a *request*
- "I need a new computer" is a *solution to a problem*

Even if they look like needs, complaints, requests, and solutions are wolves in sheep's clothing, so you must be careful not to let them into the flock!

Complaints imply needs, but they are not needs in themselves. Of course, a complaint implies that some need is not satisfied, but the need is not made explicit. It is left to the other party to guess what it might be.

In the best case, the other party is clairvoyant and correctly guesses that, when you say you need clearer reports, you're seeking to better understand the subject in question (a need that a report is unlikely to satisfy!).

Or they could be confused, and we could enter into a long, pointless conversation about how to write a report.

Or perhaps they are obliging, in which case they might waste hours polishing the document.

Or, as discussed, they could get defensive: "But my report is perfectly clear!" In this case, we have antagonized the troll, and our candid exchange has become even more difficult.

On the other hand, even though it might take a bit more thought and a few extra words, you could try something else: "I'm having trouble understanding what you're working on, and when I read this report, it's not clearer to me. To manage the project properly, I need to get to grips with this subject. However, my schedule is crazy, so I need to be extremely efficient. Let's discuss what can be done."

If you're having trouble expressing a need, you may inadvertently make a *request* disguised as a need—for example, "I need you to..." or "I need more...." This inaccurate expression is doubly frustrating for the other party since you are asking them for something without saying so explicitly and leaving them to guess why you need it!

For example, if you interrupt a meeting by saying, "I need you to move to another room," this could be interpreted in several ways. Do you mean that the room in question is critical to some important work and that something terrible will happen if you don't get it now? Or that it is needed by a VIP? Or that you consider it your right to have the room, having gone through the procedure for reserving it?

If the other party is in a lousy mood, perhaps stressed by their ongoing meeting, this ill-expressed request—which is not a need as such—could spawn problems. The fix is simple: you must just say what you mean. Instead of "I need ...", "I want you to ..." or "I would like you to ..." are more straightforward and accurate expressions, less likely to cause confusion. In addition, it would probably help to explain the intention behind your request, for reasons given earlier.

A similar and very common error is to advocate a *solution* as though it were a need.

For example, a new computer could be a solution for all sorts of problems, and statements such as "I can't get on the web again; *I need a new computer*" are wide open to counterarguments. A cooperative person might respond by trying to understand the problem and needs more details before suggesting one or two solutions. Still, in the context of a difficult conversation, the following retort is more likely: "There you go again! If you only learned to configure your network connection properly, you wouldn't get these problems!"

Why irritate the troll like this? Why not offer an explanation, rather than disguising a solution as a need? For example, "I can't get on the web again, and when I think about how many times I get stuck like this, I get down. I don't like technology, and I don't have the patience to learn how web connections work. I need a way to get my work done without bothering other people." Such a response is less likely to result in irritation and resistance and admits multiple solutions.

Needs precede solutions

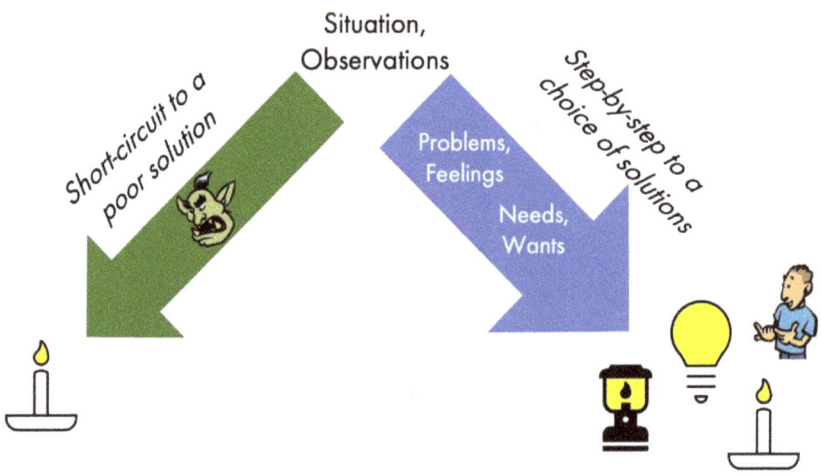

We've seen that accurately expressing facts, feelings, and needs tends to calm the emotional troll. However, there's even more to it than that.

Once emotions have settled down and the conversation returns to normal, you must start looking for a solution with the other party. This is the operational part of the discussion that follows a successful candid exchange. After you have aligned your understanding of the situation with the other person, the question that remains is this: which solution best satisfies everyone's needs?

Unfortunately, many difficult conversations don't follow the process recommended by CCC; they short-circuit the candid exchange. Instead of dealing with the troll and arriving at an understanding that includes everyone's needs, people tend to rapidly summarize the situation and propose a solution. This is an inefficient way of going about things. It not only lets emotional reasoning wreak havoc but also results in multiple, possibly superior solutions getting overlooked.

Hence, accurately expressing needs—talking about real needs, not making complaints, requests, or pushing solutions—is crucial. It not only improves the quality of a candid exchange but also helps you find a solution to the matter at hand once the candid exchange is successfully completed.

Simple formulas

The complexities of communication in a candid exchange could leave you thinking that your explanations will also be complex—in fact, the opposite is true, since it's crucial to keep things simple and avoid adding to the complexity. I will offer a few examples, based on the following straightforward sentence structures, to demonstrate this:

- I believe that ..., whereas I need ... and so I'm feeling ....
- I'm feeling ... because I want ..., whereas I understand that ....
- I would like ... but as far as I can see ... and so I'm feeling ....

The first template presents your understanding, beginning with the factual part, following with needs, and finishing with feelings. The second starts with feelings, then proceeds to needs, and ends with observations. I leave you to work out the third case shown and the six other ordering possibilities. I also invite you to practice by filling in the "..." parts based on your real or imagined experiences. Here's an example (notice that I have not followed the three templates to the letter):

- "I believe the customer has gone elsewhere, though I was counting on their order, so I'm feeling pretty miserable."
- "I'm feeling aggrieved because I place a high value on loyalty, and I understand that you've decided to join our competition."
- "I wanted the software to be working by now, but as far as I can see, there are at least two more weeks of work to do, so I'm very disappointed just now."

Here are some further templates for showing empathy:

- I see that ... has happened, whereas I believe you were expecting ..., and so I guess you're feeling ...?
- I imagine you are feeling ... because you were hoping ... would happen, but it seems that ...?
- I believe you wanted ... but as far as I can see ... and so I suppose you are feeling ...?

Here's an example based on the above templates:

- "I see that you didn't get the job, whereas I believe you were expecting it, and so I guess you're feeling a bit low."
- "I imagine you are frustrated because you hoped the meeting would happen, but it seems they've put it off for the third time."
- "I believe you wanted a BMW Series 3, but as far as I can see, you're not going to get a car at all, so I suppose you are feeling let down?"

Of course, candid exchanges can't be settled by following a formula. The intention behind these examples is to demystify the business of explaining observations, feelings, and needs. What you say does not have to be long or complicated. Furthermore, the phrases used can be even simpler than my examples if they only cover one or two of the three points, as is often the case in an actual candid exchange.

Explain as a last resort

The *Pause*, *Ask*, and *Listen* chapters precede the *Explain* one because, in many circumstances, explaining can be considered a last resort. Having paused to calm yourself and reflect, invited the other party to speak, and listened carefully, general calm may have been achieved, so there is no need to explain anything, at least as far as the candid exchange is concerned. Remember, once again, that the aim of a candid exchange is nothing more than to have the troll leave the room.

This point notwithstanding, it may be necessary to explain your understanding of the situation carefully. By discussing it last, I am not suggesting that the Explain stance is less noble than the Pause, Ask, and Listen stances. Rather, I am pointing out that pausing, asking, and listening are at least as important as explaining.

When you prepare for a difficult conversation with someone, your thoughts move naturally to what you will say to them—to your explanations. You probably spend less time thinking about your intentions and the questions you will ask and getting yourself into a mindful state, ready to pause and listen. However, my personal experience and the work I have done coaching others through challenging conversations have shown that if the other steps are not given adequate attention, the time spent on explanations is usually wasted.

A candid, calming explanation should thus be seen as a necessary but not sufficient means of persuasion. You must use it in conjunction with pausing, asking, and listening. In doing so, try to be as accurate, honest, and benevolent as possible, whether talking about observations, feelings, or needs. When you manage to do all this, there's a good chance that the troll will take his leave.

Staggered Conversations

In a staggered, asynchronous conversation, you send a message and wait. There may be no immediate reply, and if you're worried about what you wrote or troubled by an unduly slow response, the wait may seem eternal. Or perhaps, on an open forum, you're frightened that nobody will reply at all—no comment, no likes, nothing!

Conversations through email, chat, forums, and social media differ from synchronous dialogues in other ways as well. Accessibility and reach, for example: anyone can publish messages across asynchronous platforms, often reaching unknown recipients. Moreover, the responses may come from anonymous individuals or automated systems.

This broad exposure can lead to both challenges and opportunities. While you often seek visibility—if thousands of followers read your article, you'll be delighted—it can also be intimidating. You might be affected by this in different ways. If you are desperate to be liked, you might bend your subject, style, and even your opinions to please as many people as possible. In this case, you sacrifice authenticity. On the other hand, if the prospect of your work being widely viewed drives you to write more carefully, your authenticity might improve.

Computer-Mediated Communication (CMC) is a highly complex subject, and research on how people use and abuse asynchronous communication has a hard time keeping up with rapidly evolving tools and platforms.

What could possibly go wrong?

This question might have been asked by people who, around 1980, could see the potential for the electronic delivery of messages and widescale networking. The prospect of sending messages almost instantly and accessing data from remote sources offered huge advantages over the technology of the time. However, as we have learned, CMC is not all plain sailing.

Send in haste, repent at leisure

Since you receive so many messages daily, you're often hurrying to process them all. You are thus forced to write messages so hastily that you don't think enough before hitting the send button. This can cause fretting at both ends of the communication channel.

The person receiving a hastily written message, perhaps not realizing it was written in a rush and should not be taken too seriously, may agonize about its contents. At the other end, the sender, haunted by a nasty feeling that they'd not spent enough time on an important piece of communication, may ruminate about its possible effect.

While agonizing and rumination have always been a problem associated with communication—people fret about past and future physical conversations and brood over written letters for hours—the issue seems to crop up particularly frequently in CMC.

Lack of flow and timely corrections

The staggered nature of an asynchronous conversation impedes conversational flow and engagement, and differing time zones do the same.

It also prevents the correction mechanisms that we take for granted in face-to-face conversations from working well. If you say something that the other party dislikes when talking to them in the office, their immediate feedback, in the form of speech or non-verbal cues, tells you this. When remote and distant, you can be quite oblivious to the effect that your words are having.

It may be hard to build rapport

Establishing personal connections and rapport is challenging in asynchronous conversations. If people have never had the opportunity for synchronous communication, then the immediacy usually required for fostering emotional connection is absent.

Although it's possible to build a relationship only through written communication—in past centuries, there were many cases of pen-pals getting married—it's far easier when face to face.

Information overload and disorganization

Multiple threads and messages can clutter conversations on platforms such as forums or group chats, burdening you with the difficult task of tracking and organizing discussions. Moreover, the sheer volume of messages to process can leave you mentally overloaded.

Online candid exchanges

Compared with its synchronous (real-time) counterpart, asynchronous (staggered) communication has two major challenges:

First, given that people ruminate over written messages, *far fewer errors can be tolerated than in a spoken conversation*. If you make a mistake in a synchronous, verbal conversation, the other person's reaction may lead you to correct your error before it's too late. On the other hand, if your message goes out as an email or a tweet, then the damage may be difficult to reverse.

Second, *your message must provide enough context* since you have no idea when, where, or how it will land. Will it be received on a computer, a phone, in a quiet office, on the metro, in the bath, or in bed? For social media, you don't know how old another person is, their culture, their state of health, and so on. In many cases, you don't know, and can't check, how much another person knows about the subject, if they'll understand a cultural reference, or if they share your sense of humor.

With this in mind, let's have another look at the guidelines I previously offered for difficult synchronous conversations. I have modified them slightly.

Accept the situation	~~Read to confirm a viewpoint~~	
Just **read**	~~Ideate or dream~~	**READ**
Remain open-minded	~~Contemplate my next move~~	
Check my story	~~Filter or distort~~	
Address the real difficulty	~~Avoid discomfort~~	**PAUSE**
Adjust my intentions	~~Consider operational objectives~~	
Use the right channel	~~Assume they're like me~~	
Strive for perfection	~~Hit SEND before full reflection~~	**ASK**
Free the response	~~Corner the other person~~	
Share observations	~~Hide interpretations~~	
Reveal feelings	~~Accuse or confuse~~	**EXPLAIN**
Describe needs	~~Complain or try to obtain~~	

As you can see, I've only made three changes:

- I replaced "Listen" with "Read" for obvious reasons.
- I have started the list with Read and not Pause, as this seems more natural in an asynchronous context.
- I replaced "Just ask" with " Strive for perfection"—the latter has become a *recommendation* rather than a taboo!

In a synchronous setting, "Just ask" is a reminder to avoid striving for the perfect question. However, as mentioned above, only minimal errors can be tolerated in asynchronous, written communication, especially when the conversation is difficult. Hence, "Strive for perfection" is now a *recommendation,* and "Hit SEND before full reflection" is prohibited.

This point notwithstanding, it helps to remember that "Perfection is achieved, not when there is nothing more to add, but when there is nothing left to take away" (de Saint Exupéry). Hence, although you take enough time to optimize your message and delay pressing SEND as long as possible, it's best to keep it short. Using the minimum number of words reduces the risk of triggering an adverse reaction, since each word is a potential trigger. Rather than heap explanation on top of explanation in an attempt to avoid being misunderstood, it's best if you remove troublesome words in the first place.

Notice that, although the injunction "Strive for perfection" has changed sides when moving from synchronous to asynchronous conversations, the fundamental principle underlying it—try to avoid triggering an adverse reaction—remains as important as ever.

Most of the guidelines (left) and taboos (right) listed in the image above demand no further comment, since they are the same as for synchronous communication, but I would like to elaborate on a few of them in the asynchronous context.

Adjust your intentions

A simple intention to remember is "Be nice and clear."

Nice essentially means showing consideration for your recipient's feelings and time. In addition to the technical aspects of composing the message (see below), this means being honest and benevolent, as prescribed by CCC.

By *clear*, I mean difficult to misinterpret. Being "difficult to misinterpret" is a much higher standard than being "easy to understand." When you check your message for possible misinterpretations, you are forced to consider alternative points of view. If you only ask yourself, "Is this easy to understand?" you will likely conclude that it is, but only because you are the author of the message.

Use the right channel

In addition to the psychological channels described in the chapter *Ask*, you must add the dimension of technological channels when going asynchronous. Are you using email, chat, Facebook, LinkedIn, Twitter/X?

Remember that there is often a choice, and fight against the tendency to reply to a message using the channel (and copy list) it came in on. Instead, consider the audience, context, and message content, then consciously select the most suitable channel for communication.

Each channel has unique attributes that influence communication dynamics. Sometimes, especially when an asynchronous conversation has become difficult, you may even use a synchronous alternative—use the phone or send a calendar invitation for a video call, for example.

Asking and explaining

When talking face-to-face or on the phone, you usually take a few moments to exchange pleasantries. Although this serves no operational purpose, it would be unconventional and perhaps rude not to do so.

In contrast, it's best to be *upfront* when communicating asynchronously. You should provide immediate context regarding the purpose of the message, helping the reader quickly decide whether they want to read, file, or trash your message. Hence:

- If the message is just for information, you say so immediately.
- If it requests an action, you make the request immediately.
- If it agrees to something, you agree to it immediately.
- If it refuses a request, you refuse it (you guessed) immediately.

The body of the message can elaborate, if necessary, and you should not assume that anyone will read it. Above all, you must not try to trick your audience into reading everything. The tactic of placing the most important content at the end of a message—in an attempt to have its recipient read everything that goes before—is misguided.

Simplicity is the ultimate sophistication. Short, straightforward, active phrases beat convoluted ones. You write, "Someone deleted the file," rather than, "The file was somehow deleted, but we don't know by who."

You should use the present tense as much as possible—it's clearer, crisper, and easier to digest; it helps keep things simple.

You should also separate different types of content—ideas, opinions, questions, information—into separate paragraphs, using blank lines generously.

Finally, although short is usually good, too short is cryptic. You shouldn't write "<=>, >|<" instead of "Less is more, more or less," for example!

Not hitting SEND too early

Before sending, you make a three-way check:

- Is the email OK?
- Will the intended recipients be OK?
- Are you OK?

The first check is the most obvious: are the facts right, the dates correct, and so on? Are the grammar, formatting, and spelling good? Have you attached the cited documents?

Evaluating a message for appropriateness and its potential impact on recipients is even more critical. You must remember that they will receive it in circumstances unknown to you.

Lastly, you must pause again. I've found that the following rules help a lot at this point (Altucher):

- Don't press "send" when you are angry
- Don't press "send" when you are paranoid
- Don't press "send" when you are anxious
- Don't press "send" when you are tired
- Don't press "send" when you want to be liked

Social sharing of emotion

As food for thought, I would like to finish this chapter by citing work that shows how much remains to be understood about communication and emotion. It's an invitation to continue exploring this rapidly evolving subject. In fact, its evolution is greatly accelerated by the development of social media and the new communication scenarios it has created. If my breakfast porridge was cold when I was a boy, few people got to know about it. Today, I can complain to the whole planet!

Rimé et al. concluded their 2020 paper on this subject as follows (Rimé):

"It has long been ignored that emotional experiences are systematically put into the social field. The social sharing of emotions pervades everyone's daily life. [...] The fact that every emotion leads the individual to turn to others and talk about it indicates that emotional experience raises both a relational question and a question of meaning. Future studies will need to examine human adaptation in light of this perspective."

I take from this that emotions should not be ignored. Though I advocate banishing the troll from the room, since the feelings he represents prevent calm communication, this does not mean that sharing emotions is not valuable—it just has to be done carefully, as we have discussed.

This point is crucial when using social media, email, and other technologies for difficult asynchronous conversations.

As Derks explains, using CMC, "it may be easier to express negative emotions towards others because one does not know the other, or because one is less aware of the social effects of one's own expressions." (Derks)

In other words, anonymity and distance make it easier for you to be rude. However, Derks goes on to say that remoteness has potential advantages as well:

"Further, we assume that reduced visibility of emotions strengthens emotional style and content and makes it easier to express emotions, especially when individuals find it difficult to express them in real life."

Therefore, we see that while you might find it hard to express a strong emotion when you're face-to-face with another person, you can more easily articulate, for example, extreme anger or sadness through a written message. However, in case you think that you've now understood this issue, what Derk says next raises new questions:

"It may be more difficult to recognize emotions with reduced visibility, however, especially when they are not very intense."

Here, you see that, though remote communication may allow you to express strong emotions that are often suppressed when you are in someone's presence, more subtle feelings may vanish from the scene. A tiny shift in intonation or microscopic facial expression could give you valuable information when you are sitting with someone at the same table or on a video conference. Such small shifts will probably be lost when you communicate asynchronously.

Giving further support to the idea that we don't fully understand CMC, the Kurzgesagt video "The Internet is Worse Than Ever–Now What?" begins as follows (Nutshell):

"In 2022, nearly half of Americans expected a civil war in the next few years. One in five now believes political violence is justified. And it is not just in the US but around the world. People increasingly see themselves as part of opposing teams.

There are many different reasons for this, but one gets blamed a lot: social media. Social media divides us, makes us more extreme and less empathetic, riles us up, or sucks us into doom scrolling, making us stressed and depressed. It feels like we need to touch grass and escape to the real world.

New research shows that we might have largely misinterpreted why this is the case. It turns out that the social media internet may uniquely undermine the way our brains work, but not in the way you think" (emphasis mine).

In addition to explaining one or two surprising things about social media, Kurzgesagt offers pointers to its sources of information, and I recommend them to anyone wishing to understand more. For myself, I can't help thinking that all our technology and research has brought us right back to "All I know is that I know nothing," a phrase attributed to Socrates[28] (c. 470–399 BCE)!

Goodbye to the Troll

Finally, having discussed matters candidly, emotions have calmed down, and now you may address the operational issue related to the difficult conversation.

For example, consider the case of the customer concerned about supply chain issues in the Pause chapter. Suppose the candid exchange successfully achieves calm and results in both parties changing their perspectives.

You learn that your customer interpreted your earlier statements about their "special customer" status as an ironclad guarantee of priority treatment, and they told their senior management as much. Your inability to supply parts on time has, therefore, seriously compromised their credibility. However, you are able to reassure them that if there was a misunderstanding regarding product delivery priorities, it was unintentional.

Having straightened this out, the troll leaves, and you start to address the operational issue of what to do next. You identify an opportunity to bring two of the client's managers together in a meeting with you and your boss so that you can explain the supply difficulties to them and present a forecast. This should take the heat off of your customer, provide their superiors with more visibility and understanding of the supply situation, and repair relations between the two companies.

Next, let's return to the case of the black sheep in my software development team from the Ask chapter. I had used the wrong communication channel with a junior colleague and, uncomfortable receiving my barrage of questions, they clammed up (i.e., withdrew).

A few hours later, realizing my error, I had another discussion with them. Having started by explaining my intention—to help them achieve their goals and, by extension, do the same for colleagues depending on their work— I was brief and directive. I asked them to summarize recent progress for me, together with obstacles they had encountered and how they were dealing with them. It became apparent that they were getting stuck with and spending too much time on one particular task, and they seemed to realize this as they talked.

After a productive, candid exchange, I was able to proceed toward my operational objective. I fired up Excel and loaded the team's current project plan, pointing out activities where my black sheep was on the critical path. I asked them to review their plans in this light, discuss them with their colleagues, and report back to me in a few days.

Finally, let's revisit your smelly cubical cohabitant. It took a lot of patience to get Nicky to understand that the side effects of their cycle to work were distracting and unpleasant for you. You had to be especially careful not to use judgmental words ("smelly," in particular!) and avoid generalizing about what was acceptable and unacceptable in an office.

Once they'd understood that their actions were causing you a certain amount of suffering, they became less annoyed by having to discuss hygiene and promised to think about what could be done. However, the topic remains a delicate one, and should you ever need to bring it up again, you should do so with considerable care!

In all three of the above cases, the critical aspect of the conversation was the candid exchange. When it was over, the rest was comparatively easy. However, though a candid exchange can get a relationship back on track, it rarely transforms the people involved into best friends. A difficulty is resolved, but it's probably not forgotten, and it takes time before confidence is fully established or restored. Hence, even when in calm dialogue, you must be careful.

Heading off the next troll

Suppose you're in the border region where everyone is apparently calm, but emotion is fermenting and about to take over. As we've seen, the critical part of a difficult conversation is from the moment the troll enters the room until he leaves it, so it makes sense to anticipate his visit.

You can sense him knocking at the door when, for example:

1. People are stressed and in a rush.
2. A person is obsessed with proving that their view is right.
3. Nobody is talking about the troll in the room.
4. Someone's using power or manipulation to crush any opposition.
5. Most of the talking time is taken by one person.
6. Your colleague is not really listening.
7. The other party's comments are causing the hairs on the back of your neck to rise.

These unwanted behaviors are warning signs and are easily recognized, but you can't quell them by simply telling the people around you to stop being stressed and to stop being in a rush, for example. The key to discouraging them requires an *indirect* approach, one that stimulates constructive attitudes:

1. Thoughtful pauses in a discussion.
2. Openness to other people's points of view.
3. Difficult subjects being brought up and discussed courageously.
4. Participation based on honest, benevolent intentions.
5. The talking stick doing the rounds (literally or figuratively speaking).
6. Attentive listening.
7. Crisp explanations that do not provoke defensiveness.

You can, for example, encourage thoughtful pauses in a discussion by asserting yourself in the discussion calmly and making such pauses yourself. To make this explicit and noticeable, you might even say, "Just a moment, I need to think for a second," before holding a brief silence. In other words, you model behavior that you want others to adopt.

Each item in the second list is a key characteristic of CCC, and anything you can do to introduce them into everyday dialogue will tend to keep the troll away.

Prevention is better than cure, and although the appearance of a troll is usually associated with a conflict of interest or opinions, be aware that he sometimes enters the room in surprising ways.

For example, remembering and talking about emotions may cause someone to be overtaken by them. When someone explains that a mail they received triggered so much anger that they couldn't sleep all night, they may become furious while they say this, even though they were perfectly calm a few minutes before. Another person, when presenting news of a somber nature, may become worried and dismal as they do so, even though the news does not directly affect them. This is why news presenters must be made of solid stuff!

However, it is quite possible to talk about emotions without reproducing them on the spot. The idea is to *explain* them, not *demonstrate* them!

For example, when Esther Perel[29], an expert on relational intelligence, talks about the complex and strong emotions and feelings that exert such an enormous effect on our lives, she does so in a way I find enthralling. There is passion in her explanations. However, she does not cry when she talks about sadness or throw her clipboard at the cameraman when she discusses anger. Rather, she communicates her deep understanding of these emotions through her posture and choice of words. She shows enormous empathy for her audience but does not torture herself with excessive sympathy.

Similarly, George Stephanopoulos, a well-known anchorman on US television, frequently has the unhappy duty of interviewing disaster victims for Good Morning America. Doing so, he stays quite calm while showing tremendous empathy for his interviewees. One of his secrets is starting work at 2 am in order to be fully prepared for the day, ready to tackle its shocks and surprises.

While 2 am may be early for most people, George's discipline reminds us that, when preparing for an event where you know you will have to discuss or recall strong emotions, you should think about how you will handle this in advance. One way to keep the troll at bay is to process any uncomfortable feelings before the event.

A troll is like influenza. If it takes control, then you face a big struggle to return to normal. The most effective action is taken when you are well—when things are calm. You can head off the next troll by encouraging CCC in everyday conversations and anticipating emotive issues.

I contend that the CCC methodology is simpler than the Highway Code and takes much less time to learn. Therefore, given that most people manage to pass a driving test, learning the basic theory described here should present little difficulty.

However, I want you to do more than simply learn a new methodology. I would also like you to survive your first few attempts at using it and develop excellent difficult conversation skills over time. Once you've become confident at handling a wide range of difficult conversations, I'd like the methodology to continue to be a valuable reference, helping you to analyze new situations when they come up.

Getting prepared and starting safely

When you expect a conversation to become difficult, you should do as much work as possible away from the contact zone. You can pause for thought even before meeting the other party. That way, you will have revised the story you're telling yourself, focused on the actual difficulty, and decided on your intentions in advance.

Visualization can also help you when preparing. Many top athletes visualize their sprints, jumps, and throws before they actually do them. If this technique works for physical skills, it's surely good for the relatively intellectual ones involved in conversation! By anticipating how the other party might perceive the current situation, their concerns, and expectations, you prepare yourself to be sensitive and empathic.

These points about pre-meeting preparation notwithstanding, I like to remember Eisenhower's comment about plans:

> *"In preparing for battle, I have always found that plans are useless, but planning is indispensable."*

Or even Woody Allen's:

> *"If you want to make God laugh, tell him about your plans."*

In other words, preparation will help, but you must be ready to abandon your plan and adapt to the unpredicted turns an actual conversation might take.

The safest way to practice is to observe from a safe distance! Watching a film is not too dangerous, for example. Films have plenty of heated confrontation scenes, though the more spectacular ones don't resemble real life. I recommend something more subtle than Mad Max.

Meetings can also be good low-risk learning opportunities if you aren't directly involved in an ongoing confrontation and can simply observe. The more detached you are from what's going on, the easier it will be for you to watch and learn. Ultimately, you should be able to achieve a certain detachment from your own difficult conversations, and this will help you stay calmer and learn more from them.

Deliberate practice

You must practice *deliberately* to acquire new skills and obtain a targeted level of expertise. This type of practice requires focused, sustained, and systematic efforts. You should choose a specific part of the difficult conversation model to work on and review the practice experience to learn as much as possible.

To practice independently, you need something safe to work on—surgeons refine cutting skills on various inanimate objects, not live patients! You also need a reference model, using which you can monitor progress and correct your technique.

Fortunately, you already have a model. The troll, the four aspects of the candid exchange, and the guidelines for each aspect offer valuable vocabulary and structure.

For a safe testing ground, you could try writing mini-plays or film scripts in which actors engage in difficult conversations. I learned a lot from doing this, and I recommend it as a self-coaching exercise.

In the annex, you will find *Film Scene Improvisations*, and these provide an excellent starting point from which you can write your own scenes, perhaps with alternatives. You may then compare them with the full scripts and associated notes included after each improvisation.

It's also a good idea to leave scenes you have written for a day or two and then return to them. You'll be more objective about the quality of your efforts after a few days, and reviewing them will give you new ideas. Of course, you may also share your script with others and get their suggestions. You can even use artificial intelligence tools to create and review scripts.

The scenes in the annex were first employed in training classes. During training, participants were given just the start of the scenes and asked to improvise their difficult conversations from that point. They then gave each other feedback and sometimes reran the scene (which is how it works when making a film—the first take is rarely the final one).

Learning partners

Many people will find it helpful to have a learning partner, usually someone who is also developing their difficult conversation skills. Just as it's somehow easier to go to the local gym for an hour of torture when someone else comes along, so it is with working on difficult conversations. What's more, in addition to providing moral support, a partner can role-play with you, which is a particularly effective form of deliberate practice.

It can also help to have a coach: either a person with formal coaching qualifications or someone else willing to give constructive feedback and encouragement.

Everyday opportunities

Many difficult conversations start with email, with some of them being conducted entirely through this medium. You can analyze your past exchanges and learn from them or apply difficult conversation skills to live ones, taking extra time to ensure that you follow the candid exchange guidelines.

You can also use "normal" conversations for practice. For example, you can practice eliminating your tyrannical assessments from speech, expressing feelings accurately, listening actively, and so on, even if there is no particular difficulty to deal with. Making a conscious effort to apply the guidelines will help embed them as habits.

When practicing in these ways, remember that mistakes are inevitable. You will make many, and you will never eliminate them entirely. With this in mind, I include the following extract from Leonard Cohen's song, *Anthem*, to remind perfectionists like myself of the importance of letting things go:

> *"Ring the bells that still can ring,*
> *Forget your perfect offering,*
> *There is a crack in everything,*
> *That's how the light gets in."*

Anchoring with a mind map

Anchoring allows you to remember something reliably by using a mental reference such as a metaphor, an image, or a tune. For example, you might remember the number 5991 with the help of a tune in your head that starts with a note of medium pitch, rises for two notes, and then finishes with a low bass note.

This method of remembering is effective because it forces you to work with the material you wish to learn. Almost any effortful activity can be used for anchoring.

When reading a book, you are in a passive position, letting the ideas flow according to the organization of the text in front of you. When anchoring, you take an active stance since you have to think of your own metaphors, images, etc., and relate them to the material. This helps considerably with both understanding and recall.

Therefore, I recommend learning CCC by anchoring what, for you, are its most valuable parts in a form that reflects your needs and style. Why not try:

- Writing short scenes for films or plays, as described above and illustrated in the annex.
- Producing your own CCC poster and pinning it on your office wall?
- Preparing a pitch on CCC, perhaps using the TWO-MINUTE MESSAGE technique (Betts, chapter 7)?
- Creating a PowerPoint presentation capturing what you've learned. You could perhaps use Pecha Kucha ("Percha Kucha") for this?
- Using Sketchnoting to associate helpful images with words (Sketchnoting)?
- Discussing CCC with your rubber duck[30]?

A Mind Map could also be a great way to begin, so I'd like to offer the diagram below as a starting point ("Mind Map").

SOMETHING'S TROUBLING ME — 131

That's all I have for now, so I invite you to start anchoring. Have fun!

Epilogue

In a highly interconnected world, there's often a troll in the room. As human-changing technologies and indifferent exploitation of our resources relentlessly lead us onwards—if not upwards—there are plenty of difficult conversations going on.

Of course, improved global cooperation is essential to our survival, and more effective communication is key to achieving such cooperation. I was motivated to write this book by an intuition along these lines, and the writing process has brought it into sharper focus. Therefore, I hope this book will facilitate your communication efforts and that they will be directed, in a general sense, toward a better world.

ANNEX

Pictorial Summary

Emotional thinking, as opposed to rational thought, is the primary obstacle in a difficult conversation. Hence, you must restore your calm and help others do the same.

Therefore, your first objective should *not* be to solve an operational problem. It should be to find a way to better deal with the excess emotion and make everyone involved more comfortable, efficient, and effective.

You must persuade the troll to leave the room so that you can have a calm, professional conversation, allowing you to address operational issues.

Don't Panic!

When highly emotional trolls are about, people are inclined to attack others, retreat from danger, avoid issues (retreating from reality), or get confused

These *uncontrolled* fight, flight, and freeze responses are detrimental, though their *controlled* counterparts—that is, deliberate escalation, withdrawal, or delay—are sometimes useful.

You should not often resort to controlled fight, flight, and freeze, but it's essential to keep these options in mind. Sometimes, a satisfactory outcome to a difficult conversation is just not possible, given the people involved, their collective history, and the time available.

And, paradoxically, once you no longer feel obliged to bring your difficult conversation to a satisfactory end, it's more likely that you will!

Candid and Calming Communication

Candid and Calming Communication (CCC) consists of:

- A hypothesis: that restoring calm is a prerequisite to progress
- A mindset: a state of mind favoring an appropriate reaction at the onset of a difficult conversation
- A method: what to do when you see a troll.

The mindset includes:

- Positive initial assumptions (pre-suppositions)
- A systemic attitude (with a "nudge & adjust" approach)
- A combination of honesty and benevolence

When difficulties arise (i.e. a troll appears!), put operational matters aside and have a candid exchange with the sole objective of restoring calm. Do this using four stances: Pause, Ask, Listen and Explain.

Pause

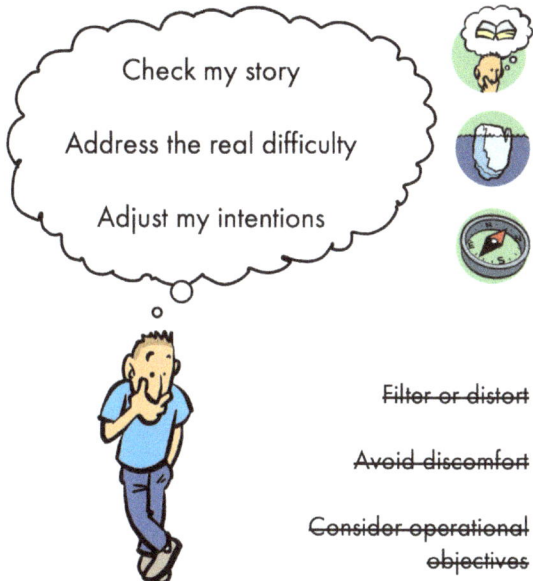

The Pause step is crucial. It is necessary to control your feelings, gather your thoughts, and *consciously* decide what to do.

"Check my story" means examining your internal dialogue, reviewing your interpretation and evaluation of what you've seen and experienced. This is not only useful preparation for a candid exchange, it is also calming.

"Address the real difficulty" invites you to identify and deal with challenging issues you would rather avoid.

"Adjust my intentions" reminds you to clarify the intentions that will guide you through your candid exchange.

To deepen your understanding of these three guidelines, consider the effect of the deprecated behaviors, shown crossed out above.

Ask

Questions determine the flow of a discussion. They shape a conversation. Hence, the way you ask the other party to contribute is crucial.

"Use the right channel" reminds you that others may not have the same communication preferences as you.

"Just ask" is an invitation to ask without delay and to use simple language, preferably in the present tense.

"Free the response" suggests asking in a way that does not make others feel cornered or forced to say things that they would rather not. The corollary to this idea is that you must accept their response for what it is, even if they decide not to reply.

Listen

Your challenge is understanding how the other party sees things, empathizing with them, and getting insight into what they fundamentally need.

"Accept the situation" directs you away from denial and rumination about the way things should be.

"Just listen" reminds you to free yourself from internal and external distractions and to listen mindfully.

"Remain open-minded" means striving to hear what the other person is saying without any premature assessment.

Explain

You and the other party need to have the same data and use the same vocabulary to describe that data. To this end, you must explain your understanding of the situation, your feelings, and your needs as *accurately* as you can. Do so in a way the other party is inclined to consider.

If you are successful, they may present their viewpoint with little prompting.

Share Observations

Looking at the objectively verifiable facts of the situation is often the best place to start since you can usually resolve disagreements in this area by looking at data. Having done this, you may share your perspective on that data.

However, this isn't as easy as it seems. When emotions are running high, it's like walking through a minefield. A misplaced word or tyrannical assessment can have catastrophic consequences.

Furthermore, although it's tempting to think you can't go wrong by sticking to facts, you must remember the dangers of brutal honesty.

Reveal Feelings

The troll represents two sets of emotional commotion: your own and that of the other party. Hence, to calm the troll, you must empathize with others while paying attention to your own feelings.

Sometimes, describing your feelings will benefit the candid exchange. However, talking about them can be difficult because you can get emotional when doing so. To overcome this, remember that your feelings are real phenomena, even though only you are directly aware of them. Try to describe them similarly to how you would describe something external, adopting the same attitude as when sharing observations.

Describe Needs

A crucial skill in difficult conversations is expressing needs that other parties can relate to. However, even if you say "I need ...," you often fail to express a real need.

For example: "I need clearer reports" is a complaint; "I need you to move to another room" is a request; "I need a new computer" is a solution to a problem.

Expressing needs accurately is crucial to a fruitful candid exchange and to finding solutions thereafter. Once people understand what's needed, the right solution tends to emerge.

Staggered Conversations

Conversations through email, chat, forums, and social media differ from synchronous dialogues. Key examples:

- Given that people ruminate over written messages, *far fewer errors can be tolerated than in the spoken word*.
- *Your message must provide enough context* since you have no idea when, where, or how it will be received. Or even who will receive it.

The guidelines associated with Pause, Ask, Listen, and Explain apply with minor changes. These stances become Read, Pause, Ask, and Explain, and your attention is drawn to the following:

- Adjusting intentions
    - Be *nice*, considering the recipient's feelings and time
    - Be *clear*, writing text that is difficult to misinterpret.

- Use the right channel
    - Fight against the tendency to automatically reply to a message using the channel (and copy list) it came in on.
- Be upfront with your message
    - If it is just for information, say so immediately
    - If it is requesting an action, make the request immediately
    - If it is agreeing to something, agree immediately
    - If it is refusing a request, refuse immediately.
- Don't hit SEND too early!

Goodbye To The Troll

Finally, having discussed matters candidly, emotions have calmed down, the troll has left, and you may address operational issues if you wish.

Remember that a difficult conversation started when the troll entered the room, so it makes sense to anticipate his next visit and keep him out.

For this reason, the guidelines outlined here are relevant to "normal" discussions and important when emotion is fermenting just under the surface.

Methodology Fundamentals

This annex reviews some of the thinking behind the Candid Calming Communication methodology. It is included here for the benefit of those interested in understanding more about its theoretical aspect.

Important Words

Let's consider some of the terms I have used to describe the type of exchange being sought: candid, accurate, benevolent, and honest. Why didn't I use, instead, frank, precise, compassionate, and true?

Candid versus frank

The most concise distinction I found between candid and frank was made by a contributor to the English Language Learners Stack Exchange forum. They pointed out that "candid" is more about saying things you would rather not say, while "frank" is more about saying things the hearer may not wish to hear.

Accurate versus precise

The quest for precision is closely associated with perfectionism, and I have already warned against the dangers of this tendency. If the precise value of a share is 51.437 euros, it is accurate and perhaps sufficient to say that its value is between 50 and 52 euros. Accurate data is correct without necessarily being precise.

Accuracy is an excellent compromise between too much precision and insufficient rigor. By settling for it when explaining your observations, you avoid going into unnecessary detail. At the same time, by aspiring to it when you try to express feelings and needs, you achieve greater clarity.

Hence, aiming for accuracy works well for all three aspects of your explanations: observations, feelings, and needs. It is a consistent and simple approach.

Benevolence versus compassion

When considering the difference between benevolence and compassion, it helps to mention empathy, also. Empathy is understanding others' feelings, whereas benevolence is wishing to help others (so that they feel better). Compassion is empathy and benevolence combined and is, therefore, a more ambitious goal. As far as resolving a candid exchange is concerned, while compassion would certainly help, benevolence is often sufficient, hence the choice of the latter word (this reasoning is similar to that used when choosing "accuracy" over "precision.")

Honest versus true

"Honest" is preferred rather than "true", since saying only what is true is *not sufficient* to achieve honesty. I can inform a colleague that they have been put forward for a job—a true statement—without mentioning that someone else is sure to get the position. The colleague was put forward only to satisfy bureaucratic requirements. This omission is dishonest.

Finally, brutal honesty is excluded by the combination of all four terms: candid, accurate, benevolent, and honest. A statement such as, "Your psychometric test results are in the bottom quartile, and we've decided to keep you in your current position indefinitely, hoping that you will eventually quit," may be accurate and honest, but it's certainly not candid or benevolent (instead, it's frank and mean).

It's not just about violence and compassion

A great deal of work aimed at improving the quality of interpersonal communication has focused on anger and the violence that this emotion can lead to. For example, the NonViolent Communication (NVC) movement leans strongly in this direction.

While I believe that NVC provides valuable guidance, I have also come to see its focus on violence as limiting. Fear, sadness, and even joy can get in the way of calm decision-making. Guilt and disgust may also confuse our thinking.

Another criticism of the term "NonViolent" is that a positive label would be more effective. After all, when we express a goal using a negative term, although we exclude something unwanted, we do not define the specific goal we're trying to achieve. Although it's clear that NVC abhors violence, it's not clear if the aim is joy, honesty, tranquility, agreement, or love, for example.

To avoid the word "nonviolent," some NVC advocates prefer "compassionate." However, as explained in the chapter *Don't Panic*, communication must be benevolent and honest (Levine). And, while compassion is even stronger than benevolence, it does not include honesty. As Kim Scott points out, if this component is missing from one's practice, there is a risk of "Ruinous Empathy™." To quote from her web page, "Ruinous Empathy is 'nice' but ultimately unhelpful or even damaging. It's what happens when you care about someone personally but fail to challenge them directly. It's praise that isn't specific enough to help the person understand what was good, or criticism that is sugar-coated and unclear."

For these reasons, I prefer the adjectives *candid* and *calming* since "candid" combines the concepts of benevolence and honesty, and "calming" suggests the aim of standing back from our emotions so that we can hear them without being overwhelmed by their noisy demands.

Nothing's perfect, however, and a possible difficulty with emphasizing the term *calm* is that, in a world where a great slogan is vital to getting one's message through, it is not a very exciting word. Isaiah Berlin[31] summarized some of his most important work on the history of ideas in 100 words[32] and then commented, "A little dull as a solution, you will say? Not the stuff of which calls to heroic action by inspired leaders are made?". He then ruefully quoted one of his contemporaries, who'd written, "There is no a priori reason for supposing that the truth, when it is discovered, will necessarily prove interesting."

Uncommon guidelines

In this book, I've advocated considerable discipline when leading a candid exchange and suggested guidelines for each of its four aspects or stances—pause, ask, listen, and explain. From among these guidelines, I would like to emphasize a few that are often missing in other texts:

- Forget your operational objectives until calm returns
- Intention trumps any technique
- Ask using the present tense
- Mindfulness is the key to quality listening
- Take a similar approach when talking about for facts, feelings and needs: explain your understanding of them as accurately as you can
- Controlled fight, flight, or freeze are always possibilities

Forget your operational objectives until calm returns

Many objectives in life cannot be achieved with a direct approach. For example, you cannot relax by *trying* to relax. Similarly, there's no point telling someone to be spontaneous—if they strive to do something, then they are not being spontaneous, so how could they try to be spontaneous?[33] Likewise, you cannot make someone trust you by simply demanding trust. People need to see concrete actions that demonstrate your trustworthiness.

An inappropriate attempt to get something directly is called "end-gaining" (Alcantara) or "striving for," and we often make this error when racing against the clock.

Another way to look at this phenomenon is to consider "process" and "result." Your to-do list is full of results that you wish to achieve: "Fix the GUI bug, Get dog food, Call Jitesh, Send Acme quote, ...". While it's natural to focus on these goals, focusing exclusively on results can blind you to the importance of process. Sometimes, attending to the process and letting the results sort themselves out is the best approach.

For difficult conversations, focusing on the process means starting with an emphasis on restoring calm (a crucial step) and thinking about operational goals (the results) only once calm has been achieved. You don't strive to get an agreement with someone when you're both distraught. You don't end-gain. Instead, trust the process, put aside your operational objectives for the moment, and focus on each stance of the candid exchange.

Intention trumps any technique

When I started giving training on difficult conversations, I worked with a handful of clients to formalize a methodology for dealing with difficult conversations in the workplace. We highlighted the need to clarify intentions in our first draft, but, at the time, I underestimated its importance. My subsequent deliberate use of the methodology soon showed the critical influence of intentions on the outcome of a candid exchange.

I have several professional activities. As a sales consultant for a large software company, I have to deal with a steady stream of difficult conversations with colleagues and clients. I also coach professionals from varied backgrounds on their communication challenges and see a wide range of cases. Without exception, since I've been paying particular attention to the intention with which a candid exchange is undertaken, I have found it critical to a successful outcome. A robust intention—clear, honest, and benevolent—has the following benefits:

- You feel more confident being candid because once your intention is clear, both to yourself and the other party, you know that you are unlikely to be misunderstood.

- If your words don't come out right, since the other party understands that you are well-intentioned, they are less likely to become defensive or aggressive. You will, therefore, have a chance to correct your mistakes
- If everything goes wrong and the conversation descends into conflict, you will at least know you approached it with a decent intention as you pick up the pieces.

Ask using the present tense

This guideline connects with the first (… forget your operational objectives …) since it forces you to focus on what's going on in the candid exchange rather than being distracted by objectives you may have for the conversation that may follow it.

The power of using the present tense is that (1) it is straightforward, and (2) it avoids much trouble. As soon as you start talking about the past, you find that others don't share your history assessment, and disagreements result. As for the future, when you ask someone to promise something, a contract is implied, and a candid exchange is no place for that. The present tense keeps you out of trouble—it is your friend

Mindfulness is the key to quality listening

"We choose to go to the Moon in this decade," said John F Kennedy in 1962, expressing a goal in clear, positive terms and providing the springboard for that effort. It's hard to set such a clear goal regarding mindfulness, which can never be fully achieved. Unlike the moon, it forever remains mysterious and elusive.

However, Kennedy continued, "…because that goal will serve to organize and measure the best of our energies and skills." The comparison with the goal of mindfulness now becomes closer, and to understand why, you must distinguish between the *process* needed to achieve a goal and the goal itself—the *result*.

The moon landing was not important in itself. Why go to so much trouble to have a couple of men take a walk on a distant rock? On the other hand, working out how to get there—inventing the process needed—helped American industry to make huge technological steps, boosting both the economy and the national mood.

Similarly, developing processes that help you towards your mindfulness goal is far more important than a particular result, such as the duration of your meditation. Striving hard to be more mindful tends to be counterproductive, like straining to sleep or endeavoring to be popular with everybody.

Given that mindfulness is a process-oriented activity, it follows that mindful listening is also process-oriented. Therefore, you must forgive yourself whenever the quality of your listening falls short and treat every listening experience as a step on the road to long-term improvement. At the same time, you must not become complacent. If you're serious about improving your listening skills, you should deliberately practice mindfulness, using sports and meditation exercises, for example.

Explain your understanding accurately

Although facts, feelings, and needs are different animals, they get mixed up in conversation. You constantly switch between data, interests, emotions, information, requirements, and so on in a fluid but unordered manner. It, therefore, helps to adhere to a single guiding principle when expressing yourself: instead of treating facts, feelings, and needs differently, you must explain *your understanding* of each of them as *accurately* as possible.

When explaining how you see a situation factually, there is always a danger that the other party will disagree with your observations. However, most disagreements can be resolved with a fact check—we can google it, check the email, call the person concerned, etc. Hence, rather than aiming at a complete and perfectly correct statement, you simply explain your understanding accurately.

The same approach works well when expressing feelings and needs, though for a slightly different reason. These are intangibles that an outside party cannot check. You are the only one with access to your feelings and needs, even though they may be indirectly observable through your demeanor. Either way, if you attempt to explain them as accurately as possible, not attributing them to any particular cause but simply describing what's happening inside you, there is little for the other party to object to. Hence, this explanation is unlikely to trigger an adverse reaction.

In the *Pause* chapter, I emphasized the need to take responsibility for your feelings and avoid Emotional Attribution Errors. When you make such an error, you are essentially saying that others are responsible for your feelings, and this is inaccurate. In this sense, aiming for accuracy —simply describing how you feel as well as you can—facilitates the expression of emotion and reduces the risk of offending others.

Similarly, in the *Explain* chapter, I described the challenge of explaining needs. Once again, you strive to explain accurately your understanding of what you need just now.

This approach to explaining, bringing to the foreground the idea that all you can do is describe your current understanding as accurately as you're able, liberates your expression. This posture allows you to say things you would not otherwise dare mention. You can say that you were confused by the data, that you don't know how to describe what you feel, although you're uncomfortable, and that you need to be reassured. And lots more.

When you skillfully share information about feelings and needs that only you can access, there is no reason for others to perceive an accusation. It allows you to express yourself firmly and move things forward.

Controlled fight, flight, or freeze are always possibilities

Finally, there is the *controlled* fight, flight, and freeze safety valve.

It's a safety valve but not a "Get out of jail free" card, so you should only use it as a last resort. Controlled fight, flight, or freeze may damage relations with the other party. However, you have to accept that some difficult conversations will not have a happy ending, and by doing so, you relieve yourself of the injunction to always "get a result."

Once again, we see that a process-oriented approach is more appropriate than a results-oriented one. If you must aim for perfection, then you should focus on executing an error-free process rather than achieving a faultless scorecard.

Common denominators

By paying particular attention to certain "common denominators," you simplify and deepen your understanding of the critical elements in a candid exchange. Therefore, I'd like to draw attention to three concepts that have come up repeatedly in earlier chapters:

- Internal dialogue
- Thinking errors
- Tyrannical assessments

Internal dialogue

Recall that your internal dialogue is what triggers the emotions you feel. When someone bumps into you in a crowd, and if you're telling yourself that this place is dangerous and that there are thieves and pickpockets everywhere, you are likely to react fearfully. If, on the other hand, your self-talk says that this place is fun and pleasantly busy, then you'll probably have a quite different reaction. Either way, the bump is just data going into an algorithm, and that algorithm is your internal dialogue. If you change it, then the resulting emotion is different.

For some reason, external stimuli tend to drown out the sensations inside us. When someone speaks to you, when the meeting heats up, or when you read an inflammatory tweet, your attention immediately shifts to these outside sources. Mindfulness training helps you overcome these distractions: it enables you to pay more attention to your inside world, including your self-talk. Such attention is not at all egoistic. Rather, it is key to dealing more effectively with the outside world[34].

Here are some places where self-talk has an impact on a candid exchange:

- When pausing for thought, as described in the *Pause* chapter when discussing the story you tell yourself.
- When asking or explaining something, your internal dialogue is like a rehearsal of what you say out loud. For example, if you tell yourself that your client's situation is a mess, the words "this mess" could slip undiplomatically into your words.
- While listening to someone, your internal dialogue will undoubtedly be contaminated by built-in filters and biases. If you are aware of those filters and biases, you can correct this (to some extent). For example, if you know that you tend to blame your children's laziness for everything that goes wrong for them, you can try to listen to their excuses with a more open mind.

Finally, note that a candid exchange can start *and end* with self-talk if the troll in the room is entirely of your own making. For example, suppose you read an email, and your emotions immediately go into the red. If, after (1) reviewing the story you're telling yourself, (2) considering the real difficulty, and (3) deciding on your intention, you calm down and see that the best course of action is no action at all, then your candid exchange is over before it began!

Thinking errors

Here are some examples of where thinking errors may have a significant impact on different aspects of a candid exchange:

- When you take a pause to check your story and consider the difficulty at the heart of the conversation, thinking errors can lead you to misunderstand the situation you're dealing with. For example, by making confirmation errors, you may ignore valuable evidence (because it contradicts your pre-existing opinions).
- Similarly, when listening to the other party, thinking errors trigger distracting emotional reactions. The error may begin with the other person. Suppose they say, "HR upset everyone with their

announcement," this attribution error (blaming HR for people's reaction to the announcement) could fire your emotions.
- When getting ready to ask or explain something, you must also be wary of thinking errors since, as previously discussed, such errors strongly affect what we say.

In all these cases, mindfulness is tremendously helpful. It allows you to recognize errors more quickly and to keep your thinking on the straight and narrow.

Kahneman and his colleagues have performed many fascinating experiments to demonstrate a wide range of thinking errors (Kahneman). They show how you can make them spontaneously and how people may attempt to manipulate you into making them. Either way, watching out for them is well worth the effort!

Tyrannical assessments

Interpretations, evaluations, and predictions can easily become tyrannical assessments, with their unfortunate consequences, as discussed. However, you would quickly become overwhelmed if you did not assess incoming information. Interpretation allows you to compress incoming data into something you can comfortably remember, and making assumptions speeds up the interpretation process. You then evaluate the processed information to understand its implications—what it means and might predict. If you did not evaluate and predict, then you would simply be acting as a storehouse for interpreted data.

The challenge is to make subjective assessments as consciously and accurately as possible and to remain able to return to first-order, raw data—what you saw and heard—when necessary.

The critical point is to be *conscious* of your interpretations, evaluations and predictions. If you make suppositions, projections, interpolations, hypotheses, etc., that's fine as long as you recognize that's what you're doing. Similarly, you may generalize or apply some homemade rules to quickly assess a situation, providing that you do this consciously.

With this in mind, let's look at places where tyrannical assessments affect a candid exchange:

- When pausing for thought, unconscious interpretations, evaluations, and predictions affect the story that you're telling yourself, and reassessing them is key to gaining an alternative view of your situation and, with luck, calming yourself. Whatever clarity you can achieve will automatically affect your assessment of the real difficulty in this challenging conversation and condition your intentions for tackling it.
- Our core guideline for listening to the other party is "just listen," so it follows that interpretation, evaluation, and prediction must be postponed while the first order, raw data is brought on board. You must delay assessing, or it will interrupt your listening. A direct consequence is that you must interrupt the speaker sometimes—"Excuse me, I need to think about what you just said. Do you mean that …" for example. If your capacity for raw information is exhausted, you must process it before going on.
- When asking the other party something or explaining something to them, unconscious subjectivity may cause you embarrassment when your incorrect understanding of the situation becomes evident to the other party. Worse, they can pollute what you say, triggering an adverse reaction. "Because of the 10% increase …" might be an acceptable thing to say, for example, but "Because of this huge increase …" might provoke irritation or anger—"huge" is a judgment!

Summary

By emphasizing the need to achieve calm before dealing with operational matters, CCC brings a fresh approach to difficult conversations. At the risk of sounding dull, its description does not include emotive terms such as violent, compassionate, and radical, for example. Such terms might encourage emotional reasoning, which, as I have argued, is the root cause of difficult conversations!

Although none of the guidelines associated with the four aspects of CCC are new discoveries, several of them are not often mentioned, and I have drawn attention to these rarities in this annex.

Finally, an important feature of CCC is that its four aspects share certain common principles, a firm grasp of which will help you bring clarity and simplicity to your difficult conversations.

Lights, Camera, Action!

List of scenes

1. Resisting politely
2. Saying what you want
3. Dealing with resistance
4. Expressing discontent
5. Asserting your personal interests
6. Giving bad news
7. Facing irritation and anger
8. Asking for more commitment
9. Addressing unwanted behavior
10. Confronting a peer about repeated issues
11. Confronting a collaborator about repeated issues
12. Giving thanks

Setting up

Why not have some fun while practicing difficult conversations? By supposing that you are directing or playing in a film scene, you can try out candid exchange tactics painlessly. If the scene doesn't work out well on the first take, you can just "cut" and try again.

The twelve scenes provided here are presented first as scenarios and initial scripts from which improvisations can be created. You can write your improvisation down, record it, or act it out in a group, for example. Group work can be done in the context of a training course or with friends and colleagues.

Another possibility is to use an artificial intelligence (AI) tool to generate a script and then review it (alone or with others). Scene 1, take 2, gives an example of this approach. Conversely, you could write a script and ask an AI tool to review it.

In addition to the improvisation scenarios, full examples of candid exchanges based on each of the scenarios are given at the end of each scene section. These may be treated as examples that supplement those given earlier in this book or as suggestions with which to compare the improvisations that you come up with. Notes are included to explain each script.

However you decide to use the material, it will help you anchor the concepts discussed earlier and adapt those concepts to your needs and style. As Seneca[35] recommended, dare to try things and make mistakes because you will learn faster that way.

For simplicity, the context of all the film scenes is the same, and it is described on the next page, together with the cast of characters. In each of the scene descriptions, this context is reduced to the minimum necessary to understand the scene, and only participating characters are mentioned. In addition, guidelines are provided to the "director" of the scene. They explain its purpose, give some ideas on how to guide the actors, and, occasionally, invite the director to take the part of a minor character in the scene.

To further help the director and to support group work and training, the section *Film Scene Facilitation* gives facilitation guidelines.

Enjoy!

Film Scene Improvisations

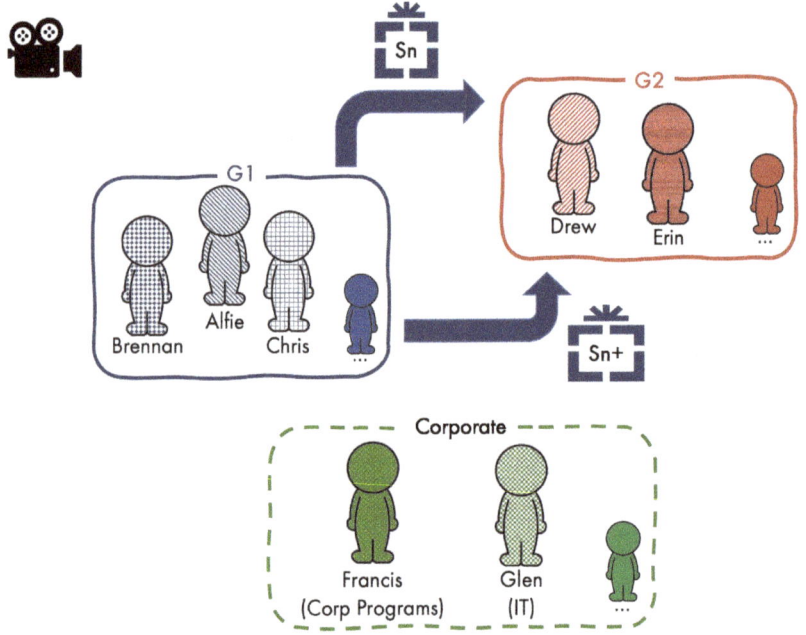

Note: the undersized character in each group represents unnamed members.

Context

Group G1 has developed several Solutions recently, the latest being Sn+. They believe that it has huge potential and wish to promote it to group G2 for use in their products and services. This would mean revenue for G1 and it would also validate Sn+, giving it credibility and helping it to succeed in other markets.

G2 is already using Sn, an older Solution from G1, though integrating it was an unhappy experience. There were delays, and relations between the two groups became strained.

The term "Corporate" is used to refer to the company as a whole, excluding G1 and G2.

Cast of characters

Alfie, Brennan's and Chris's boss (Manager-Leader in G1).

Brennan, An Engineer (Individual Contributor in G1—reports to Alfie).

Chris, An Engineer (Individual Contributor in G1—reports to Alfie). Very competent though always joking about, trying to do many things at once, rarely on time.

Drew, Erin's boss (Manager-Leader in G2). Conscientious. Holds strong views on *how* things should be done but is more flexible on *what* should be done.

Erin, An Engineer (Individual Contributor in G2—reports to Drew). Technocratic, logical, organized; impatient with others who don't see things as clearly as them.

Francis, A Corporate Program Manager (Manager-Leader in Corporate). Results-oriented. Charming and persuasive. Has a tendency to push people into competitive positions (i.e., slightly manipulative).

Glen, An IT Engineer (Manager-Leader in Corporate). Technically masterful. Tormented by conflicting desires for speed and perfection.

Scene 1: Resisting politely

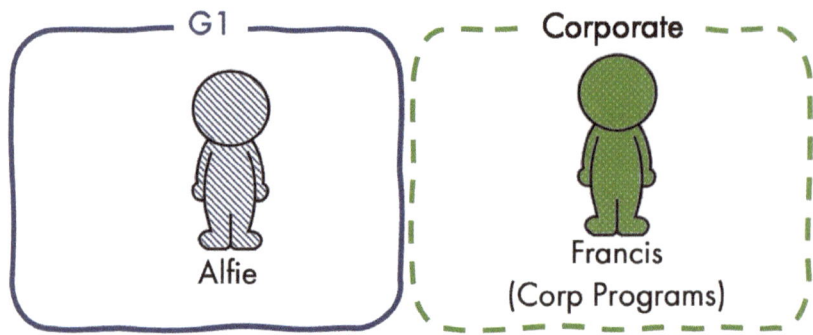

Alfie has been working on a presentation for an important meeting with G2 for the past three weeks. They sent Francis a complete version for checking two weeks ago and have been regularly mailing and calling them to ask for feedback. Francis has been unresponsive.

The meeting in question is tomorrow, and it's 6 pm when Francis calls...

Improvisation starting point:

Francis: Hi Alfie, do you have a minute?

Alfie: Sure, I'm just finishing up for the day, but I've got a few minutes. What's up?

Francis: I just went through the presentation that you sent me for the inter-group call tomorrow. I like it a lot, but I think you should add backup slides with details of the Sn+ results that you told me about.

Alfie, improvise from here using the following information:

The current presentation is already quite long.

Alfie and Francis have already agreed that, for this meeting, the priority was to get an agreement in principle and to avoid getting lost in technical details. Even so, there is some merit in Francis's suggestions.

Francis, improvise from here using the following information:

You are a Corporate Program Manager, a Manager-Leader in Corporate.

React naturally to any troubling language from Alfie (defensively or by becoming dictatorial, for example).

Director, *to help the actors with their improvisations, note that:*

The purpose of this first scene is to warm up participants to the film metaphor and to demonstrate moving toward the real difficult and starting with the right intention. Maybe sharing observations, too.

For the improvisation, cut whenever the scene could be improved, then rerun. You can even try variants that are WORSE than the original improvisation—there is nothing wrong with a Director who experiments!

Interesting variants could be, for example:

1. Alfie says, "Sorry Francis, I've got something on tonight. I can't do it."
2. Alfie says, "Francis, I've been calling you for weeks about this. Now you're asking for changes at the very last minute. You're stressing me out! I've said I'll be home by 6h30, so I can't fix it tonight, no way. Sorry."

Script suggestion (take 1):
Francis: "Hi Alfie, do you have a minute?"
Alfie: "Sure, I'm just finishing up for the day, but I've got a few minutes. What's up?"
Francis: "I just went through the presentation you sent me for tomorrow's inter-group call. I like it a lot, but I think you should add backup slides with details of the Sn+ results that you told me about."
Alfie: "Er Francis ... *takes a few seconds to think* ... before I answer, I have a question [1]. I'm a bit perplexed, and I'd like to clear the air before we talk about the presentation. Is that okay?" [2]
Francis: "Sure. Is there a problem?"
Alfie: "Well, after I sent the slides a couple of weeks ago, I sent at least two emails and left a voicemail. Did you get these messages?" [3]
Francis: "Yes, I think so. But I've been so busy that I've just not had time for this. Sorry!"

Alfie: "Okay. I guess I was expecting you to jump on the slides as soon as I sent them, and that wasn't realistic. I'm disappointed, but I can live with that." [4]

Alfie: "Now, about the presentation ... I think we agreed to concentrate on the business case for Sn+ and try to get another meeting with G2 to discuss details. I can see the sense in having backup slides, but I don't have time to do them. It's 6 pm, and I promised to get home by 6:30 today. What other options do you have?"

Francis: "None. But it shouldn't take you long. Don't you have some material you could throw together quickly?"

Alfie: "Sorry. I would have to start from scratch. I'm afraid my answer is 'no,' Francis. I'm not prepared to work on this tonight."

Francis: "Could you get Brennan to do something?"

Alfie: "My policy is to never ask the team to do something I'm not prepared to do myself, so I don't want to ask Brennan." [5]

Francis: "What can we do then?"

Alfie: "Well ... [thinking] ..." [6]

... Alfie and Francis discuss potential compromises and ways to incorporate the necessary details without working late ...

Notes:

[1] Alfie is annoyed because they haven't received feedback. They identify this difficulty when they pause, and then they move towards it. This begins the candid exchange. If Alfie had not had the presence of mind to pause for thought, they might have argued with Francis about their late request for changes to the slides or given in to the request and felt bad about it, for example.

[2] They explain their intentions to Francis to ensure clarity. This is a precaution—Alfie is concerned that if they do not state their intentions explicitly, they might be misunderstood.

[3] Alfie takes a factual, unprovocative approach to expressing their disappointment at not getting feedback from Francis.

[4] Francis apologizes and explains. There is no evidence that Francis has acted maliciously, and so Alfie leaves it at that.

[5] Alfie takes full responsibility for their refusal by using the first person as much as possible (e.g., "I think we agreed...", "I promised...", "I'm not prepared to...", "My policy is ...", etc.)

[6] The exchange has allowed Alfie to express themselves and Francis to step back from their original, enthusiastic request (realizing that what he's asking for is not so easy), and they discuss options calmly and professionally.

Script suggestion (take 2):

Francis: "Hi Alfie, do you have a minute?"

Alfie: "Sure, I'm just finishing up for the day, but I've got a few minutes. What's up?"

Francis: "I just went through the presentation that you sent me for the inter-group call tomorrow. I like it a lot, but I think you should add backup slides with details of the Sn+ results that you told me about."

Alfie: "Francis, I've been reaching out for your feedback for weeks, and now, the day before the meeting, you're suggesting changes. It's frustrating, and I had plans to leave on time today." [1]

Francis: "Alfie, this is about making Sn+ shine. We need those backup slides for impact. Can't you and your team put in a little extra effort to ensure success?"

Alfie: "Francis, my team has put in their best efforts, and I respect their time. Asking them to work late on short notice is not something I'm comfortable with. Let's explore alternatives that don't compromise quality." [2]

Francis: "Alfie, we can't afford to miss this opportunity. Sn+'s success is on the line, and we need those slides to seal the deal. Can't you make an exception just this once?"

Alfie: "Francis, it's not about exceptions. It's about respect for my team and their work-life balance. I won't ask them to work late, and I won't do it either. Let's brainstorm a solution that doesn't involve late-night work."

Francis: "Alfie, time is ticking, and I need those slides. This is the big break we've been waiting for. Can't you prioritize Sn+'s success?"

Alfie: "Francis, I am committed to Sn+'s success, but I won't sacrifice professionalism and team well-being for a last-minute request. Let's figure out a compromise that respects everyone's efforts."

Francis: "Alfie, you're being too rigid here. We need those slides tonight. No excuses. It's crucial for the success of G1 and Sn+."

Alfie: "Francis, I hear your urgency, and I'm willing to collaborate on a solution. Perhaps we can find a way to integrate the key details without compromising the team's schedule. Let's work together on this." [3]

Francis: "Fine, but make it quick. We can't afford any delays. Sn+'s success depends on it." [4]

... Alfie and Francis discuss potential compromises and ways to incorporate the necessary details without working late ...

The second take was produced by ChatGPT, an artificial intelligence engine. I gave ChatGPT the scene description and a detailed description of the personalities, objectives, and constraints of Alfie and Francis. Several iterations were required; the main task was to guide Alfie's responses, "teaching" this character to respond according to the guidelines presented in this book. Francis is described as results-oriented and, though charming and persuasive, they lose their temper quickly. When they do so, they are aggressive.

Notes:

[1] Compare this with take 1. In this second take, Alfie does not explain their intention. Neither take is wrong. Think about the advantages and disadvantages of each.

[2] Alfie takes a robust stance without being aggressive. Congratulations ChatGPT!

[3] Alfie has repeated their position three times. Each time, they indicate that they are listening and understand the importance of the request, then they suggest working on a compromise.

[4] Finally, Francis seems to acknowledge the need for discussing a compromise.

Scene 2: Saying what you want

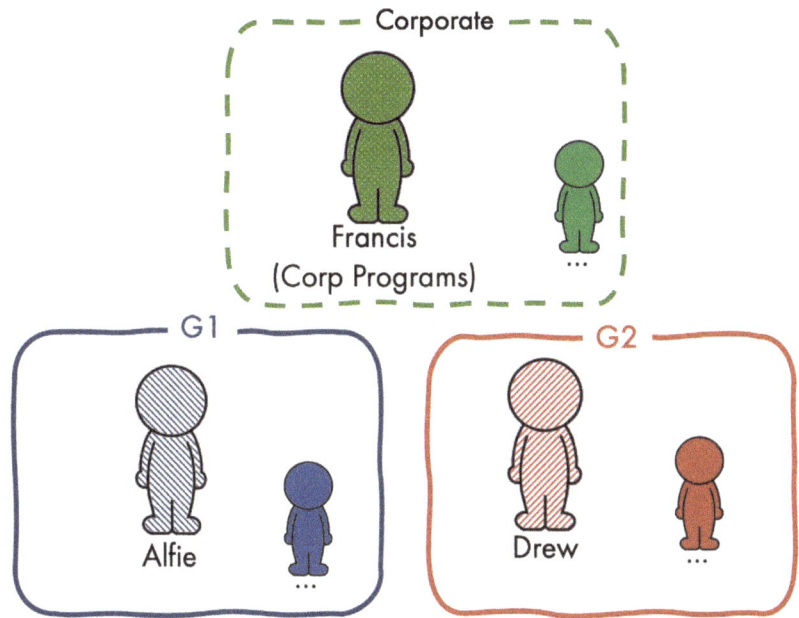

The quarterly inter-group operations review and Francis is the chair. There are about 20 senior people present in an atmosphere of inter-group politics and large egos.

Alfie wants to get an agreement for the use of Sn+ in G2 (this is the key message in their presentation, which Francis called about yesterday evening).

However, it's late into this two-hour meeting, and Alfie has not yet had a chance to talk about Sn+. Frustrated, they decide to interrupt ...

The meeting is already underway as we join it ...

Improvisation starting point:

Francis: Moving on then, I'd like to hear from Nolan about their project. Nolan, what do you have for us please?

Alfie: Francis, could I just interrupt for a moment?

Francis: Sure, but please keep it quick as we only have twenty minutes left.

Alfie, *improvise from here using the following information:*

G1 has an agenda slot at the very end of the meeting, but everything's running late.

Sn+ development is going great! It's a month ahead of schedule, in fact, and "internal beta" testing is complete. It includes all the features of Sn and some more.

Its auto-configuration feature means that it needs about a week for product setup, compared to about a month for Sn.

To maintain momentum, G1 wants G2 to agree to a "customer beta" deployment of Sn+ in their group.

If this is not agreed today, then a decision could be delayed until the next inter-group review :-(

Francis, *improvise from here using the following information:*

You are a Corporate Program Manager, a Manager-Leader in Corporate.

Compared to G1, most other groups have higher revenue, more people, and more projects—if time is short, you, therefore, tend to give them a higher priority in your meeting. Not long ago, there were delays when G2 ran a "Sn customer beta" for G1.

Drew, *improvise from here using the following information:*

You are Erin's boss, a Manager-Leader in G2.

How can G1 support a new "customer beta" when they are still sorting out the mess of the last one??

The added value of Sn+ over Sn is unclear.

In spite of past problems, you respect G1 and their expertise.

Director, *to help the actors with their improvisations, note that:*

The purpose of this scene is to highlight the importance of flexibility. Alfie went into this meeting with the aim of getting an agreement for the use of Sn+ in G2, but things did not work out as planned. How do they manage this? If you act in this scene, take Francis's part.

Script suggestion:

Francis: "Moving on then, I'd like to hear from Nolan about their project. Nolan, what do you have for us, please?"

Alfie: "Francis, could I just interrupt for a moment?"

Francis: "Sure, but please keep it quick, as we only have twenty minutes left."

Alfie: "Yes, of course. You see, G1 has a slot at the very end of this meeting, and since we are behind schedule, we're not going to be able to contribute if we continue with the original agenda. But we'd like to share some news about Sn+. Please, can we juggle things around so that we get our slot?" [1]

Francis: "Hmm, I don't know. We must talk about Poseiden and the only other slot before yours is from G2."

Drew: "Yes, and we've prepared stuff to talk about too …"

Francis: "With due respect, Alfie, other groups have a much bigger revenue footprint than you guys, and we need to hear from them."

Alfie: "I appreciate that, and I promise to keep it short. Three minutes."

Francis: "Two."

Alfie: "Thanks. Sn+ development is a month ahead of schedule—internal beta testing is complete, and so, to avoid wasting this headstart, we need to start customer beta deployment ASAP. We know that we caused G2 some pain last year when they integrated Sn, but we've learned from that. I'm asking for a meeting where we can show you in detail what we've achieved recently and decide together whether a customer beta makes sense." [2]

Drew: "How can G1 possibly support a new customer beta when we are still sorting out the mess of the last one? Also, we don't know anything about Sn+."

Alfie: "Agreed, and that is why I'm asking for a meeting." [3]

Francis: "It sounds reasonable, Drew."

Drew: "Okay, why not? Can we move on now? …"

… the conversation continues …

Notes:

[1] In spite of their frustration, Alfie avoids interpretations. They do not say the meeting is "running very late," for example. Nor do they say that Sn+ is "making great progress" or that the auto-config is "much faster" than in the past. Also, their request is straightforward (Just ask!).

[2] Alfie makes the request as concise as possible using the absolute minimum information.

[3] Alfie is guided by their intention of postponing the discussion they wanted to another meeting (a controlled freeze). They did not get distracted or reply to Drew's remarks; they simply used them to reinforce the request for a separate meeting.

Scene 3: Dealing with resistance

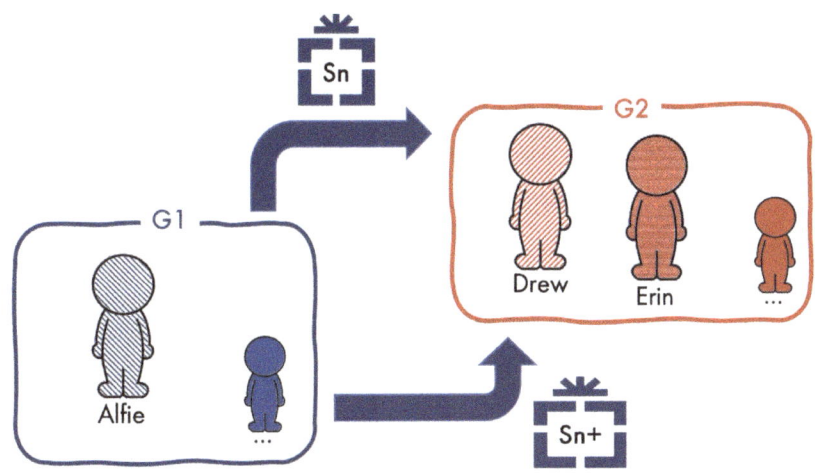

Alfie managed to schedule a meeting with G2 to discuss Sn+ deployment in their group. We are in the requested G1-G2 meeting, discussing a possible Sn+ pilot project in G2.

The G2 people are wasting time, seeing more obstacles than opportunities, focusing on trivia, and making it difficult for Alfie to talk about the main topic.

G1's objectives for the meeting are to obtain agreement for the pilot project or, if that is not possible, at least avoid a definitive "no."

The meeting is already underway as we join it ...

Improvisation starting point:

Erin: "If we start working with Sn+, we're going to have to update all our IT packages."

Drew (worried tone): "That would be a pain. We all know how long IT changes take ;-)"

Erin: "Do you know if Glen is going to be able to support us for the IT update?"

Drew: "I think so, but they were very cagey about when they could start. 'Only saw them for a couple of minutes, at the coffee station with Indigo."

Erin (sarcastic): "Ah-ha! The infamous Indigo. Well I just hope they don't get put on the job!"

Drew: "Indeed. The last time I met Indigo ..."

Alfie, improvise from here using the following information:

There were configuration problems on the last project with G2, using Sn.

In G1's defense, many of these were caused by G2 engineers not following guidelines properly.

Your understanding is that time-to-market is key for G2.

Sn+ can be reconfigured 10x faster than Sn.

G1 has used a new documentation system, and so its user manual has improved.

Erin, improvise from here using the following information:

You are an Engineer, an Individual Contributor in G2, reporting to Drew.

While the problems seen when integrating Sn were painful, you are not against Sn+. But it must be better than Sn, and there must be evidence that lessons were learned from the previous G1-G2 project.

Drew, improvise from here using the following information:

You are Erin's boss, a Manager-Leader in G2.

You are not in the mood for a pilot project with G1.

G2 has to go fast while maintaining high-quality standards—when they make a mistake, it can affect millions of users.

Director, to help the actors with their improvisations, note that:

The purpose of this scene is to illustrate how passive resistance can be dealt with. Faced with this type of resistance, how can you get everyone back to calm, professional dialogue? If you are acting, take Drew's part.

Script suggestion:

Erin: "If we start working with Sn+, we're going to have to update all our IT packages."

Drew (worried tone): "That would be a pain. We all know how long IT changes take ;-)"

Erin: "Do you know if Glen is going to be able to support us for the IT update?"

Drew: "I think so, but they were very cagey about when they could start. 'Only saw them for a couple of minutes at the coffee station with Indigo."

Erin (sarcastic): "Ah-ha! The infamous Indigo. Well, I just hope they don't get put on the job!"

Drew: "Indeed. The last time I met Indigo ..."

Alfie: "Drew, sorry to interrupt. Can we get back to the main topic, please?" [1]

Drew: "Yeah, sure. As I was saying earlier, I can understand that you want to get Sn+ deployed, but we've enough problems to deal with right now, and we're short of resources. Integrating new Solutions takes time—there are processes to follow ..."

Erin (a bit impatient): "And I'd add, Drew, that we're still reeling from the problems integrating Sn."

Alfie: "So, if I understand correctly, you are unusually short of resources and a bit sore from our last adventure together. Is that it?" [2]

Erin: "Not only that. It's unclear what advantage we would get from integrating Sn+, even if we could do it."

Alfie: "Ok. And is there anything else we should deal with in addition to these 3 points?"

Erin: "They're the main ones, I guess."

Alfie: "In that case, could I start by talking about the reasons why we think you'd benefit from doing an Sn+ pilot? I promise that we'll deal with resources and track record after." [3]

Erin: "Sure."

Alfie: "Thanks. The key advantage for you is ..."

... the conversation continues ...

Notes and questions:

[1] Drew and Erin know G1 wishes them to accept Sn+, and they are reluctant. However, instead of discussing the reasons for their reluctance frankly, they are listing as many potential problems as they can think of. This is frustrating for Alfie, who wants to get to the heart of the matter. In the face of G2's problem orientation, they attempt to have a candid exchange.

[2] Alfie tries to understand and acknowledge people's concerns before attempting to put their own arguments.

[3] With their permission ("could I start by talking about ..."), Alfie guides the audience towards a topic that is future/solution-oriented), to get away from the resistance, problem focus and negativity.

Scene 4: Expressing discontent

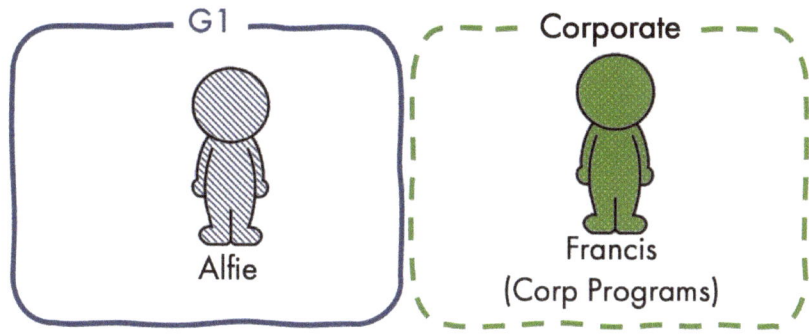

A few weeks later, Alfie got an agreement from G2 for a Sn+ pilot project.

That's great news, but Alfie then learns that the entire cost of the pilot, including G2's part, will be transferred to G1. This decision is irreversible and came about after negotiations between the CEO, the head of G2, and Francis, the Corporate Program Manager.

Alfie's just received this bad news. They're still furious when Francis calls about another matter …

Improvisation starting point:

Francis: "Hi, Alfie. Do you have a couple of minutes to talk about the schedule, please?"

Alfie: "Hi Francis, sure. But there's something else that I'd like to deal with first. I just learned that G1 has to pay for the Sn+ pilot—so G2 will cross-charge us for all their resources working on it. Is that right?"

Francis: "Yes, that's right. It was agreed on Tuesday night."

***Alfie**, improvise from here using the following information:*

G2 has sold > 50 million parts with G1's Sn. As a result, G1 received $2-3M while G2 gained 10x more!

Your first reaction: furious! The cost transfer is outrageous, and so is the secretive way it happened. Also, it puts an unfair financial burden on G1, a small group.

You had been looking forward to working with G2 in partnership—two teams meeting challenges together, sharing the risks, the spoils, and the glory. Now ... :-(

Francis, *improvise from here using the following information:*
You are a Corporate Program Manager, a Manager-Leader in Corporate.

Director, *to help the actors with their improvisations, note that:*
The purpose of this scene is to illustrate how to express discontent in a professional manner, avoiding concealed interpretations and evaluations.

Give as much help as possible to the person acting Alfie. You may have to cut the scene often in order to highlight interpretations and evaluations. That's ok—you will be critiquing the improvised script, not the person acting.

Script suggestion:

Francis: "Hi, Alfie. Do you have a couple of minutes to talk about the schedule, please?"

Alfie: "Hi Francis, sure. But there's something else that I'd like to deal with first. I just learned that G1 has to pay for the Sn+ pilot—so G2 will cross-charge us for all their resources working on it. Is that right?" [1]

Francis: "Yes, that's right. It was agreed on Tuesday night."

Alfie: "Well, I'm upset. According to the last figures, G2 has sold over 50 million parts that include our Sn component, and they take 90% of the margin. Given this amount of profit from our last project together, why should *we* pay for *their* resources on the follow-up?

Francis: "Sorry you feel that way, but it's standard procedure."

Alfie: "Then standard procedure seems unfair to me, and I'm suddenly much less confident in how this project is going to turn out. I want to feel that we are working in partnership with G2—that we have common goals and share risks. Brothers in arms and all that. I don't see this happening now [2]. Can anything be done?" [3]

... the conversation continues ...

Notes and questions:

[1] Alfie checks the facts to start with.

[2] They start with factual observations and then explain feelings and needs. They avoid concealed interpretations and evaluations and do not accuse anyone. Hence, Alfie does not give Francis any reason to become defensive.

[3] The request (Ask) is not particularly strong in this case since Alfie is facing a *fait accompli*. However, expressing their discontent has allowed them to calm down. The troll has left the room, so they are in a better position to talk with Francis about the schedule.

Scene 5: Asserting your personal interests

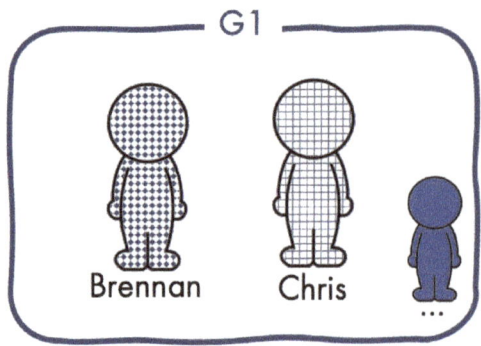

Now that G1 has an agreement for the Sn+ pilot in G2, we are now in the heart of a G1 meeting to decide who will do what.

Chris, who has spent most of their three years in G1 focused on Solutions and who has worked more than anyone on Sn+, has just made a strong case for taking the lead role in the pilot. Brennan, who has been in G1 for five years and has experience not only in Solutions but in a range of other stuff, also wants to take the role.

Everyone in the meeting can sense the tension between these two colleagues.

The meeting is already underway as we join it…

Improvisation starting point:

Chris: "… and so I really think that I would be the best person to lead the pilot."

Brennan, *improvise from here using the following information:*

You want to lead the pilot. You are interested in project management and are actively developing project management skills.

You are not only more experienced than Chris, but you are also 15 years older (40 vs 25). Though fun to work with, Chris seems anything but serious, with a surgically attached smartphone and a very short attention span.

However, if you were to lead the pilot, then you would certainly need the technical expertise that Chris has accumulated on Sn+ ...

Chris, *improvise from here using the following information:*

You are an Engineer, an Individual Contributor in G1, reporting to Alfie.

You definitely want to lead this project—it would be fun!

Director, *to help the actors with their improvisations, note that:*

The purpose of this scene is to illustrate how to assert one's own interests in a professional manner, avoiding interpretations and evaluations.

As for the previous scene, give as much help as you can to the principle actor – this time it's Brennan. You may have to cut the scene often in order to highlight interpretations and evaluations. That's ok—you will be critiquing the improvised script, not the person acting.

Script suggestion:

Chris: "... and so I really think that I would be the best person to lead the pilot."

Brennan: "I agree that, of all the people on the project, Chris has by far the most experience on Sn+ [1]. At the same time, I believe non-technical skills play a key role in project leadership [2]. I've led a couple of pilot projects in the past, and I'm invested in developing my project management skills. And although I do not have Chris's deep knowledge of Sn+, I've been working on Solutions for over a year [3]. I like that Chris is motivated, and (turning to Chris) I like working with you, Chris. For this reason, I feel awkward about pushing back against your proposal [4]. It's important to me that we work well together [5]. How would you feel about working with me as the lead?" [6]

... the conversation continues ...

Notes:

[1] Brennan starts by acknowledging Chris's arguments (presumably, their technical capabilities and relevant experience).

[2] Brennan takes responsibility for their opinion instead of stating a rule, such as "Good non-technical skills are essential in project leadership".

[3] Factual observations which are difficult to deny and which are unlikely to result in any adverse reaction.

[4] Expression of feelings. Probably, Brennan's trickiest task is identifying and expressing their real feelings.

[5] Expression of needs.

[6] A simple Ask, inviting the other person to speak.

Scene 6: Giving bad news

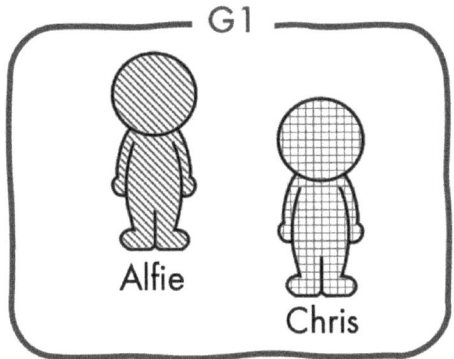

The issue of who would head up the Sn+ pilot was taken offline from the last meeting, and now Alfie has decided to give the role to Brennan.

Knowing that Chis is not going to like it, Alfie breaks the news ...

Improvisation starting point:

Alfie: "Chris, can I have a word with you?"

Chris: "Sure."

Alfie, *improvise from here using the following information:*

You've decided to ask Brennan to lead the pilot project. In your opinion: Chris is very gifted in technical matters but doesn't seem to attach much importance to the non-technical aspect of professional life.

Chris, *improvise from here using the following information:*

You are an Engineer, an Individual Contributor in G1, reporting to Alfie.

You would not be surprised if the job of leading the pilot project went to Brennan because of their age and the experience bullet points on their CV :-(

However, they know far less about Sn+ than you and are less technically competent. Technical expertise is a key quality that you look for in people.

Director, *to help the actors with their improvisations, note that:*

The purpose of this scene is to look at dealing with a situation where one's words are likely to trigger uncomfortable emotions in someone else.

Pay attention to the balance between honesty and benevolence shown by the Alfie character, and cut the scene if you think this could be adjusted.

Script suggestion:
Alfie: "Chris, can I have a word with you?"
Chris: "Sure."
Alfie: "When you piped up in the meeting yesterday and asked for the lead of the pilot, I was pleased. However, I'm afraid that my decision has gone in Brennan's favor, even though you made a good case. I imagine that you're disappointed?" [1]
Chris (unhappily): "I guess that's the word."
Alfie (slightly playful): "And there are others?" [2]
Chris: "Well, I guess that I'm a bit pissed off too because, in spite of age and experience and everything, I don't see why Brennan will do a better job than I could."
Alfie: "So, would you like to know why I decided to give Brennan the lead?" [3]
Chris (emphatically): "Yes, I would!"
Alfie: "Well, I'm not going to talk about Brennan in their absence, as I'd like everyone on the team to know that I don't discuss them with their teammates. It's a matter of principle for me. I don't talk to the others about you, and vice versa, okay?"
Chris: "Okay."
Alfie: "Okay, so it comes down to why I don't think you're ready to lead a pilot yet. The thing is, as far as I know, all your training and experience are in technology, and when I see you and listen to you, especially in meetings, I have the impression that you attach little importance to non-technical subjects."
Chris: "I don't like bullshit if that's what you mean."
Alfie: "Are you accusing me of bullshitting you?"
Chris: "No, I'm just agreeing with you."

Alfie: "I'm reassured then :-) Now, to run a project, you have to be at ease handling, let's say, things that defy a simple answer ;-) As I said, I was pleased when you made a bid for the project lead. I like working with people who have ambition, and I'd like to help you achieve this particular ambition the next time the chance comes up. So, what's your take on working with issues where there's no simple answer?" [4]

... the conversation continues ...

Notes and questions:

[1] Alfie avoids announcing the bad news brutally, without any preliminaries, but they don't delay unnecessarily either.

[2] It doesn't sound as though Alfie has prepared a speech! Maybe an opening phrase, but from then on, they let things flow.

[3] Before explaining their reasons, Alfie checks that the other person wishes to hear them. If they don't do this, they may sound defensive—as though anxious to justify something.

[4] The last point notwithstanding, Alfie respects candid exchange principles to guide what they say: no hidden interpretations or evaluations; use of empathy to understand the other person's situation/perspective, problems/feelings, and needs; endeavoring to accurately/truthfully express their own situation/perspective, problems/feelings, and needs.

Scene 7: Facing irritation and anger

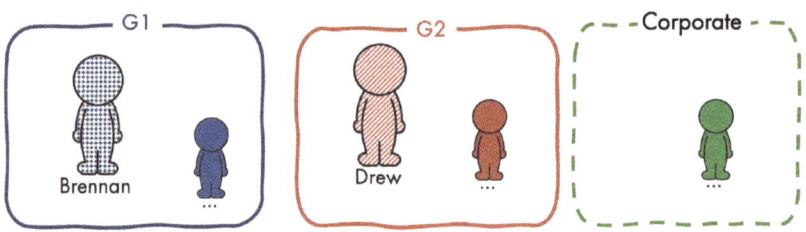

The project is underway, and inevitably, there are problems.

This is a weekly operations review. It's routine, but Drew seems to be upset about something. The G1 team's objectives are simply to report progress and sync up with G2 and IT (the latter is inactive in this scene).

The meeting is already underway as we join it...

Improvisation starting point:

Brennan: "Hi everyone. Sorry that I'm a bit late."

Drew (taciturn): "Hi, Brennan. Glad that you've turned up. You're late, for sure, but it's not just a couple of minutes that I'm worried about. Where's this release that you promised me? That's over a week now!"

Brennan: "There's been no update since yesterday, and I think that you were copied on the mail. Our best guess is the 17th."

Drew: "BEST GUESS??! I've just about had enough of best guesses! Can't you guys do better than that? This is a customer-facing project, I'd like to remind you. And it's our BU that's in the firing line! IT'S NOT F&?#@%$ing GOOD ENOUGH!"

Alfie, improvise from here using the following information:

You intend to ask Drew to provide more data on their system. You need it in order to fix some issues and give them the next release.

Drew, improvise from here using the following information:

You are Erin's boss, a Manager-Leader in G2.

You have been under pressure from your boss to provide detailed project progress information on a regular and frequent basis, and you dislike that kind of work intensely.

The boss seems to have promised regular, elaborate reports to the customer, which is stupid since G2 doesn't have the people, time, or tools to do that sort of thing :-(

Knowing the customer, they probably don't trust us to deliver on time, and that's the real source of all this hassle.

Director, *to help the actors with their improvisations, note that:*

The purpose of this scene is to work out how to deal with someone who is extremely upset.

If Brennan's response to the situation calms Drew, let the scene run. But if Drew shows signs of getting more upset, cut the scene and try to improve it.

Script suggestion:

Brennan: "Hi everyone. Sorry that I'm a bit late."

Drew (taciturn): "Hi Brennan, I'm Glad you've turned up. You're late, for sure, but it's not just a couple of minutes that I'm worried about. Where's this release that you promised me? That's over a week now!"

Brennan: "There's been no update since yesterday, and I think that you were copied on the mail. Our best guess is the 17th."

Drew: "BEST GUESS??! I've just about had enough of best guesses! Can't you guys do better than that? This is a customer-facing project, I'd like to remind you. And it's our Business Unit in the firing line! IT'S NOT &?#@%$ing GOOD ENOUGH!"

Brennan: "Okay, I'm listening." [1]

Drew (slightly calmer): "This is crazy. I can't keep going to my management and announcing new delays."

Brennan: "Your boss is giving you a hard time?" [2]

Drew: "Pressure is coming right down from the top. They're all getting jumpy about the customer seeing our dirty laundry."

Brennan: "Dirty laundry?"

Drew: "Well, I think my boss promised some kind of fancy project tracking, which we haven't got ;-). Their assistant then put together an Excel sheet, and they're pushing me for data to fill it."

Brennan: "Ouch! That must be uncomfortable."

Drew: "Too right it is!! I hate this stuff." [3]

... the conversation continues with Drew in a calmer mood ...

Notes:

[1] Sometimes, there's nothing to do but listen and wait. All other objectives are put on hold until Drew calms down completely so that they can resume a normal, professional conversation.

[2] Once Drew calms down slightly and it becomes possible, Brennan takes the opportunity to ask a question.

[3] Of course, this example is short. In real cases, it can take much longer for the conversation to get back to normal.

Scene 8: Asking for more commitment

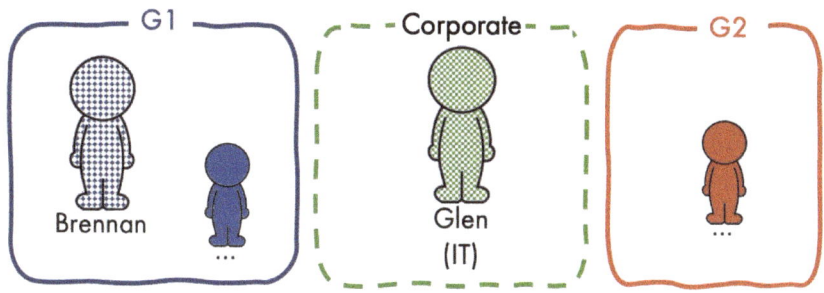

Later in the same operations review, Brennan raises some issues with IT. They have been worrying about and losing sleep over it for a couple of weeks, and their patience with IT is wearing thin.

We rejoin the meeting ...

Improvisation starting point:

Brennan: "I'd like to talk about the beta that we requested a few meetings back."

Glen: "I thought that was done now. You've had the release, haven't you? I forget. Perhaps we sent it to G2 and not you?"

Brennan, *improvise from here using the following information:*

You're furious, and you want Glen to update and reinforce IT's commitments to the pilot project.

Glen, *improvise from here using the following information:*

You are an IT Engineer, a Manager-Leader in Corporate.

Since you first promised the beta release, two IT members have fallen seriously ill, and another has gone on paternity leave six weeks before it was expected.

New work has also come up lately, associated with a new film studio project.

Director, *to help the actors with their improvisations, note that:*

The purpose of this scene is to explore situations where commitments are not being met and where getting them met is key to future work.

Look out for signs that Brennan either lets irritation show through or is too amenable. Aim for a scene that shows a good balance between understanding and assertiveness.

Script suggestion:

Brennan: "I'd like to talk about the beta that we requested a few meetings back."

Glen: "I thought that was done now. You've had the release, haven't you? I forget. Perhaps we sent it to G2 and not you?"

Brennan: "Indeed. G1 received the beta two days ago, on the 4th, whereas the original ETA was the 23rd. However, our original request was for a synchronized release to G1 and G2, and this has not happened. When I contacted IT about this, I discovered that different people were responsible for the G1 and G2 betas. And neither of them could tell me what were the plans of the other. I am confused and worried that IT delays will become a critical issue. Can you tell us what's going on?" [1]

Glen: "Well, we are very short on resources, so I had to split the beta job between two people. We're doing our best with what we've got!"

Brennan: "So what's happened? Have you lost people?"

Glen: "Not for good, but we have two people sick—quite seriously—and another on paternity leave, much earlier than expected."

Brennan (just listening): "Anything else?"

Glen: "Well, yes. When we gave you the date of the beta release, we hadn't heard about the work for the new film studio, and that's all extra."

Brennan: "Okay, I can understand that it's difficult keeping up with the extras when you're down on people [2]. However, I don't recall you saying anything about resource difficulties in our weeklies. I'm still worried and pretty annoyed, to be honest. There are a lot of people contributing to this project, and I want to be able to trust all of them to either meet their commitments or alert me if they cannot. It's much more fun that way! You know what I mean? Am I making sense?" [3]

Glen: "Er, yes, I guess so. 'Sounds like a good approach. What can I say?"

Brennan: "Perhaps you could give us an update on IT's release schedule, with any risks and caveats ..." [4]

... the conversation continues ...

Notes:

[1] Brennan starts by sharing their observations and revealing their worry and confusion. Their intention is not only to confront Glen but also to better understand what's going wrong so they don't go too far before prompting Glen to explain what's happened.

[2] Brennan listens and demonstrates that they are listening ('Okay, I can understand ...').

[3] Brennan describes their needs in some detail. They are not accusing. We could argue that "a lot of people" is a judgment and should be replaced by a completely objective statement (e.g., "there are 26 people working on this project, on average, this month, and 33 if we include contractors and the cleaning lady") ... but let's not be too picky :-)

[4] Having explained their dilemma, Brennan feels calmer. Glen is perhaps relieved at having this difficult subject out in the open without feeling attacked. The troll leaves the room, and the conversation turns to how these problems can be fixed.

Scene 9: Addressing unwanted behavior

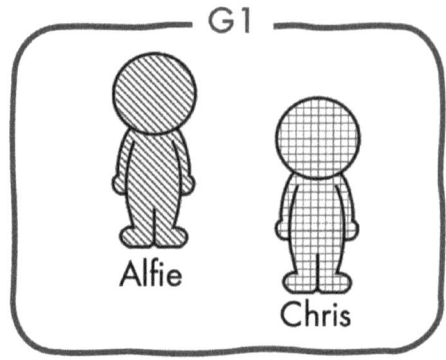

Complaints have been received from G2 about Chris's behavior. There are no performance issues, but inevitably, the project has encountered technical problems, and G2's discomfort with Chris's style leads them to attribute the difficulties to Chris.

For Alfie, the stakes are high: their relationships with both G2 and Chris are in the balance.

Chris has a tendency to joke around a lot and to tease people. They are multi-tasking and look after "private interests" (such as Instagram and music forums) in parallel with work activities.

Improvisation starting point:
Alfie: "Hi Chris, how did the meeting with G2 go yesterday?"
Chris: "Oh, fine."
Alfie: "Did Drew or Erin not raise any issues with you?"
Chris: "Yes, but nothing particularly new. There's the automatic configuration software that is still giving problems and …"
Alfie: "That's ok! Thanks. It's not what I was referring to."
***Alfie**, improvise from here, using the following information:*
Drew called to complain that they'd seen Chris "playing" on their mobile in a meeting yesterday. You request an explanation with a view to working out how this behavior can be improved. Ideally, you would like to have Chris discuss and resolve these issues with G2.

Chris, *improvise from here using the following information:*

You are an Engineer, an Individual Contributor in G1, reporting to Brennan and, ultimately, to Alfie.

Sure, you look at your mobile during meetings, but you are able to listen to what is going on at the same time.

The meeting that Alfie is referring to was no big deal anyway. They were going around in circles on some technical details of little importance.

Director, *to help the actors with their improvisations, note that:*

The purpose of this scene is to illustrate a conversation where a person is receiving information that is very likely to trigger a defensive response.

Look out for anything Alfie says that triggers a defensive response from Chris. If you see such a reaction, cut and rerun the scene.

Script suggestion:

Alfie: "Hi Chris, how did the meeting with G2 go yesterday?"

Chris: "Oh, fine."

Alfie: "Did Drew or Erin not raise any issues with you?"

Chris: "Yes, but nothing particularly new. There's the automatic configuration software that is still giving problems and …"

Alfie: "That's okay! Thanks. It's not what I was referring to. Drew called me this morning to complain. They mentioned a couple of technical issues, but the complaint cited you in particular. Drew said that they had seen you "playing"—their words—on your mobile rather than paying attention to the meeting. They said that it was hardly surprising that the project had so many technical problems. Again, these are their words. I imagine that you're surprised to hear this. Perhaps it's a bit upsetting. Am I right?" [1]

Chris: "I'm flabbergasted! Why didn't they say something at the time? I wasn't doing any harm. Even if I check my mobile from time to time, I can still listen to what's going on in the meeting!"

Alfie: "So you were using your mobile. What for?"

Chris: "I don't know. Mail, Instagram, fact-checking, all sorts of stuff."

Alfie: "Okay. In fact, I find this difficult since, like Drew, I get irritated when I see people in meetings concentrating on their phone or their laptops. Were you aware of Drew's irritation?" [2]

Chris: "No. Well, yes, a bit, I guess. But they didn't say anything."

Alfie: "Are you familiar with volcanos and their tendency to erupt unexpectedly?" [3]

Chris: "So you're saying that I should have felt the tremors?"

Alfie: "Exactly. Now, I want to give you and all members of the team as much independence as possible. At the same time, I want us all to show our clients—such as G2—respect and sensitivity. I'm pleased that you feel the tremors but not so pleased that you ignored them. What do you intend to do about Drew's complaint?" [4]

... the conversation continues ...

Notes and questions:

[1] Alfie shares the facts as they have been reported. Inevitably, this will trigger uncomfortable emotion for Chris, but they should not feel they are being accused by Alfie.

[2] Alfie reveals their feelings on the matter.

[3] Knowing that Chris has a sense of humor, Alfie lightens things up while still making an important point.

[4] Alfie describes their needs and finishes with an Ask, allowing Chris plenty of room for their reply (the request is not cornering).

SOMETHING'S TROUBLING ME — 195

Scene 10 : Confronting a peer about repeated issues

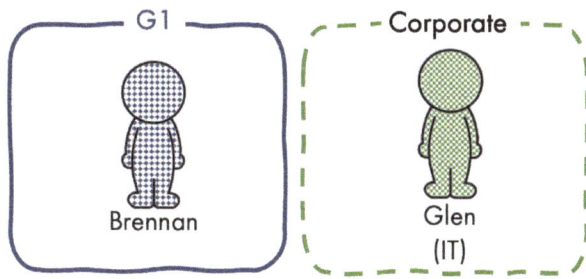

A month has passed by since Brennan's confrontation with Glen in Scene 8 and there will be another weekly tomorrow. Brennan still sees issues with IT support. Is this ever going to be sorted out?!!

Feeling their emotions running high, Brennan decides to talk to Glen one-on-one before tomorrow's meeting.

Improvisation starting point:

Brennan: "Hi Glen, How are you doing? Do you have a few minutes?"

Glen: "Hi Brennan. Fine thanks. Yes sure. How are you?"

Brennan: "Good too, thanks. Glen, I'm calling to talk to you about the schedule, and I thought that it would be better if you and I had a chat about it before tomorrow's weekly."

Glen: "'Sounds ominous ;-)"

Brennan, *improvise from here using the following information:*

Brennan's objectives are to better understand why there has been no improvement since they last confronted Glen and to find a way out of this mess with them.

Brennan can point to lots of specific issues [make some up!]

Glen, *improvise from here using the following information:*

You are an IT Engineer, a Manager-Leader in Corporate.

Everybody is asking you for things and expecting that they can be done straight away.

If you give realistic timescale estimates, then you get attacked immediately, and if you give optimistic ones, then you get attacked later, when dates slip ;-)

It's impossible to schedule things accurately because too many unexpected things come up. For example:

- The synchronized beta release fell victim to employee illness and paternity leave.

- External consultants messed up the SharePoint database.

- G1 and G2 communicating through Teams, but Microsoft changed something ...

Director, *to help the actors with their improvisations, note that:*

The purpose of this scene is to illustrate the need to make simple requests and not to demand a commitment for future behavior. It can also highlight the importance of correctly identifying the main difficulty—in this case, the *repetition* of issues.

Cut and retake to direct the scene so that Brennan addresses the real issue and makes receivable requests.

Script suggestion:

Brennan: "Hi Glen. How are you doing? Do you have a few minutes?"

Glen: "Hi Brennan. Fine thanks. Yes sure. How are you?"

Brennan: "Good too, thanks. Glen, I'm calling to talk to you about the schedule, and I thought that it would be better if you and I had a chat about it before tomorrow's weekly."

Glen: "'Sounds ominous ;-)"

Brennan: "Well, the thing is, I'm seeing a pattern [1]. Several times recently, G1 has asked for a delivery of some sort—like the one for a beta release. You've agreed to it and given us a date, then there are delays, and then I get involved directly with your guys. We then have some difficult conversations at the weeklies, you update your commitments ... and we go around again. I've noticed this happen four times recently, and I wonder if it won't happen again tomorrow. I feel the same way when I have to tackle my kids about doing their homework ;-) When they finally get it done, it's not them that's exhausted, it's me! But coming back to us, it would take a load off of my mind if I could feel confident that things were going to happen as we planned them. How do you see things?"

Glen: "Well, now that you mention it, I guess there is a bit of a pattern. The trouble is that we're forever getting surprise demands and resource problems. The ground's moving beneath us!"

Brennan: "But surely, if you are *regularly* getting unexpected problems, then they're not really surprises, are they? Do you see what I mean?"

Glen: "Not really. A surprise is a surprise!"

Brennan: "Well, if I understand what you're saying, you're almost certain that issues will come up, but you don't know what they'll be in advance."

Glen: "Exactly. There's always something!"

Brennan: "So this is a bit like saying that we know there will be bends in the road; we just don't know exactly where they will be. So why do we schedule our work as though the road were going to be dead straight?"

Glen: "Because everybody wants things done straight away! If we'd told you that the beta was going to take three months at the outset, you'd have gone mad! And, what's more, if you'd pressed us to justify "three months," we wouldn't have been able to because we didn't know what was around the next bend!"

Brennan: "So you're saying that the problem is not just the bends in the road, it's people like me, always in a hurry?"

Glen: "Yeess. I'm not blaming you particularly. Everyone's the same ... thinking ... I guess we give optimistic estimates to get people off of our backs so that we can get on with the work."

Brennan: "That's interesting. I'm glad that we're having this conversation. Can we talk about how to fix this for both of us?" [2]

... the conversation continues ...

Notes and questions:

[1] Brennan has a choice: they can either (1) raise the issue of Glen's most recent delay or (2) deal with the more fundamental problem of the pattern of repeated issues. Notice that the most important decision was taken before talking to Glen, when Brennan decided that their intention was, together with Glen, to resolve the problem of the pattern.

[2] The candid exchange begins in a straightforward way: Brennan shares observations, reveals feelings, and describes needs. In spite of this, Glen is still rather defensive. It takes some patience and several more exchanges before Brennan sees the light at the end of the tunnel, "Can we talk about how to fix this for both of us?"

Q. What might have happened if, instead of, "How do you see things?" Brennan's first request had been, "Please, can you make sure that we don't continue to see this pattern of repeated issues?"

Q. What might have happened if Brennan had started by discussing the most recent issue instead of the pattern of behavior?

Scene 11: Confronting a collaborator about repeated issues

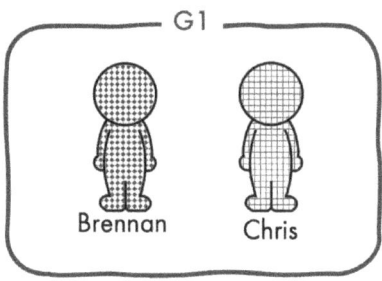

Chris is working hard and productively. However, they are repeatedly missing agreed commitments. Brennan is frequently surprised (and irritated) to learn that Chris is doing unplanned work and that tasks they agreed to do have been put off. When tackled on this, Chris invariably has a good reason for their actions, but never knowing quite what Chris is up to, Brennan finds it very hard to coordinate work across the project team.

The call is already underway as we join it ...

Improvisation starting point:

Brennan: "... Well, I'm glad to hear that things are going better with Drew. Now, have you managed to fix the Transmitter configuration yet? Case 4088?"

Chris: "No, I've dropped that for now. G2 reported an issue in the Receiver—it's been dropping packets again, more or less at random—so I've been trying to sort that out."

Brennan: "But the last time we spoke, case 4088 was *top priority!*"

Chris: "I thought that keeping G2 happy was top priority! I can't help it if the Receiver's gone crazy—it wasn't my fault! There's a workaround for 4088, but the Receiver issue's blocking. Surely it's got to have priority?"

Brennan: "Yes, but ..."

Brennan, *improvise from here, using the following information:*

There are 24 engineers working on this project at the moment in G1, G2, IT, and external companies, and it's a nightmare trying to coordinate them all.

In your opinion, Chris is unreliable, even though the work they do is of high quality.

Chris, *improvise from here using the following information:*

You are an Engineer, an Individual Contributor in G1, reporting to Brennan and, ultimately, to Alfie.

You enjoy the work that you do and the freedom to decide what's important and what isn't.

Brennan gets a bit upset about project administration sometimes, but they shouldn't worry because you know what you're doing.

Director*, to help the actors with their improvisations, note that:*

The purpose of this scene (similar to the previous one but for different circumstances) is to illustrate the need to make simple requests and not to demand a commitment for future behavior. It can also highlight the importance of correctly identifying the main difficulty—in this case, the *repetition* of issues.

Cut and retake to direct the scene so that Brennan addresses the real issue and makes receivable requests.

Script suggestion:

Brennan: "... Well, I'm glad to hear that things are going better with Drew. Now, have you managed to fix the Transmitter configuration yet? Case 4088?"

Chris: "No, I've dropped that for now. G2 reported an issue in the Receiver—it's been dropping packets again, more or less at random—so I've been trying to sort that out."

Brennan: "But the last time we spoke, case 4088 was the top priority!"

Chris: "I thought that keeping G2 happy was top priority! I can't help it if the Receiver's gone crazy—it wasn't my fault! There's a workaround for 4088, but the Receiver issue is blocking. Surely it's got to have priority?"

Brennan: "Yes, but ... pauses for thought [1] ... Reset. I apologize—I'm getting a bit upset. When you told me that you'd dropped 4088, I wasn't so much annoyed by having this case put on hold as by the fact that you hadn't warned me earlier. What happened?" [2]

Chris: "Well, Erin sent me an email about some weird behavior in one of the tests. There we some screenshots ..."

Brennan: "Hold on. That's not what I meant. My question was more, why didn't you warn me?"

Chris: "Oh, well, it was urgent ..."

Brennan: "Is that the only reason for not warning me?"

Chris: "Yes, of course."

Brennan: "It would have only taken you a few seconds to send me an email—less time than we have been talking for. Is there no other reason that you didn't warn me?"

Chris: "Well, I guess that I didn't want a debate about what to do. I just wanted to get on with it."

Brennan: "I can understand that when you're faced with an urgent technical issue, and you know how to fix it, the last thing you want is to discuss what to do with me. On my side, I'm more than happy when people show initiative, as it makes my life a lot easier. However, I also need to understand what's going on in the project since each engineer's actions affect all the others in some way. There are 24 engineers working on this project at the moment in G1, G2, IT, and external companies! In fact, I'm finding it quite hard to keep track of all the people and tasks, and I'm worried that I might miss something important soon. So, more than anything else, my interest is in helping you—and everyone else—to get on with their jobs. How does what I've just said affect your views about what to do when something urgent comes up?"

... the conversation continues ...

Notes and questions:

[1] Brennan senses their annoyance and, using this feeling as a warning sign, pauses for thought. They might be asking what story they are telling themselves about Chris, what the real problem is, and what their intention should be.

[2] Brennan seems to have managed their intentions and decided to focus on the issue of Chris not giving a warning when they switch priorities, rather than get bogged down in the mire of what happened for each individual switch.

Q. Can you locate where observations, feelings, and needs are expressed in the dialog?

Q. At the beginning of the scene, Chris seems quite defensive and on edge. Can you imagine one or two things Brennan might have said that would have caused the conversation to descend into conflict?

Scene 12: Giving thanks

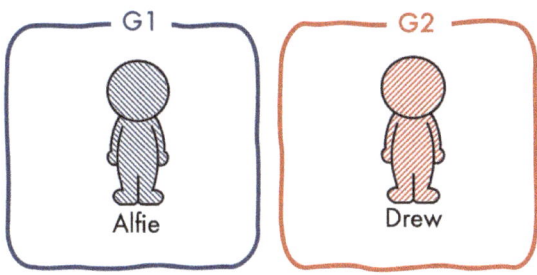

Finally, the pilot project has been a success and Drew turned out to be an excellent ally ...

Improvisation starting point:

Drew: "Hi Alfie. So we did it then!"

Alfie: "Yup! Signed, sealed, and delivered! I trust that the high-ups in G2 are pleased?"

Drew: "They are ecstatic! You know, they had doubts at one point."

Alfie, *improvise from here, using the following information:*

The thing that particularly pleased you about Drew's contribution to the project was that they showed solidarity for the multi-organizational pilot project team, defending G1 against their G2 bosses even when G1 was having trouble delivering functioning software on time.

Drew, *improvise from here, using the following information:*

You are Erin's boss, a Manager-Leader in G2.

Director, *to help the actors with their improvisations, note that:*

The purpose of this scene is to show that CCC is not only for dealing with difficulties!

Script suggestion:

Drew: "Hi Alfie. So we did it then!"

Alfie: "Yup! Signed, sealed, and delivered! I trust that the high-ups in G2 are pleased?"

Drew: "They are ecstatic! You know, they had doubts at one point."

Alfie: "And you gave us tremendous support in that sticky period, Drew. I saw you sticking up for G1 to your bosses, even when we were giving you late deliveries of broken software. I love being in a team where everyone pulls together, particularly one like ours, with so many organizations involved. The way you behaved helped me keep up my enthusiasm during our 'Darkest Hour.' Thank you." [1]

Drew: "Thank you, Alfie. That's nice to hear. Very Churchillian too :-)"

Alfie: "Well, I'm glad that we got this chance to chat. Do you know what you're going to be working on next ..."

... the conversation continues ...

Notes:

[1] Alfie is using a technique that works well for giving positive feedback: starting with the "actions" part (explaining what was done), then linking these with needs (that were fulfilled), and finally with feelings (which resulted from the satisfaction of needs). That is: Drew sticking up for G1 (action); being in a team that pulls together (needs); enthusiasm (feelings). The overall effect is to create feedback that is easier to receive and more memorable (hence, more effective) than a Thank You with little explanation.

Film Scene Facilitation

The above material was developed for coaching and training groups. I hope you find the following guidelines helpful if you wish to use them for this purpose.

Purpose

The purpose of the film metaphor and the improvisation-based process is to:

- Provide a common thread for role plays throughout a program
- Have a basis for the student's independent work and auto-correction of that work (by comparing their ideas with the examples given, for example)
- Flexibility in the learning process: Facilitators can do all the improvisation work in live sessions, students can do it all independently, or a combination of live and independent options can be used.
- If several facilitators are animating a program, make it easier for them to take a coordinated approach.
- Have fun!

Roles

In each scene, either Alfie or Brennan are facing a challenging situation, and someone must take this role. Usually, this is a student, but the facilitator may also take the role for demonstration purposes.

In addition to Alfie or Brennan, there is at least one other character in each scene to be taken by other students and/or the facilitator.

Someone must also take the role of Director. This is usually the facilitator.

Finally, students who have not been assigned any of the above roles automatically become Assistant Directors. Their role is to help the

Director improve the scene by giving feedback and suggestions at the end of each take. They should be told, for example:

- Your contributions are crucial to everyone learning from and improving the scene.
- Watch carefully, then make suggestions on how the next take could be improved.
- Take notes that can be used for debriefing after the improvisations.

General facilitation notes and guidelines

The scenes can be run using various tactics:

- Improvise, cut, and replay, asking the Assistant Directors for suggestions to fix things.
- Improvise, cut, then pick up the scene from the cut point to highlight specific points.
- Play from the example script in order to illustrate a particular learning point (this can be mixed with the above two methods also).

Scene-by-scene facilitation guidance

Scene 1: Resisting politely
This scene is often dealt with in plenary.
The main difficulty: Alfie has trouble responding rationally because they are very upset that Francis did not respond to earlier requests for feedback and that they now call at the last minute. Focus on helping the actor playing Alfie to identify their difficulty and intention.

Scene 2: Saying what you want
The main difficulty: The meeting has not gone according to plan, and Alfie's original objective of obtaining agreement from G2 for their use of Sn+ is no longer possible. Therefore, Alfie has to adjust their

intention—just getting an agreement for a later meeting is probably appropriate (a controlled freeze).

Alfie has to be assertive.

This improvisation will probably be used early in the program, and so the various theoretical concepts associated with a candid exchange may not have been discussed yet. In this case, it may be used to sensitize participants to issues that will be addressed later.

The facilitator usually plays Francis. Exceptionally, because it makes sense for the scene, there is a third actor: Drew. Their contribution is to represent G2 since, whatever Alfie decides to ask for, they will need G2's agreement.

Scene 3: Dealing with resistance

The main difficulty: In the face of G2's problem orientation, staying focused on the objective. Further, since the problem orientation is a sign of passive resistance, knowing how to deal with this (careful listening, not rushing in with one's own arguments and requests).

The facilitator usually plays Drew. Exceptionally, because it makes sense for the scene, there is a third actor: Erin. Their contribution is in the time-wasting conversation with Erin at the start of the exchange, reflecting G2's reluctance for the project being discussed.

Scene 4: Expressing discontent

The main difficulty is staying factual when emotions are running high. Avoiding tyrannical assessments.

The scene can also be used to illustrate and *sensitize* participants to the importance of dealing with emotions (if the feelings/needs aspect of the candid exchange has not been covered yet in the program).

Scene 5: Asserting your personal interests

The main difficulty is staying factual when emotions are running high. Avoiding tyrannical assessments.

The scene can also be used to illustrate and sensitize participants to the importance of dealing with emotions (if the feelings/needs aspect of the candid exchange has not been covered yet in the program).

Scene 6: Giving bad news
The main difficulty: staying factual when emotions are running high. Avoiding tyrannical assessments.
Also, showing empathy—the need to combine honesty with benevolence.

Scene 7: Facing irritation and anger
The main difficulty: faced with someone who is extremely upset, returning to a normal, professional conversation.
People tend to do too much in these circumstances, attempting to find the right thing to say. If it goes well, the improvisation should lead participants to the conclusion that listening is the key skill in this type of situation.

Scene 8: Asking for more commitment
The main difficulty is dealing with someone who, you feel, has let you down and, making things more difficult, where you will need their support in the future (hence, there is a need to strengthen the relationship).

Scene 9: Addressing unwanted behavior
The main difficulty is expressing feelings and needs clearly in a situation where there is a high risk that your words will not be interpreted as you intend.
Also, showing empathy—the need to combine honesty with benevolence.

Scene 10: Confronting a peer about repeated issues
The main difficulty is avoiding a request of the type "try to get something'. In this situation, it is tempting to ask for a commitment to do

things better in the future. Such a commitment, even if it is conceded, is unlikely to be met. So what do you request?

The scene also shows an important point about identifying and moving towards the main difficulty—not the last issue that came up, but the fact that issues are coming up repeatedly.

Scene 11: Confronting a collaborator about repeated issues

The main difficulty is avoiding a request of the type "try to get something". In this situation, it is tempting to ask for a commitment to do things better in the future. Such a commitment, even if it is conceded, is unlikely to be met. So what do you request?

As for the previous scene, this one also shows an important point about identifying and moving towards the main difficulty—not the last issue that came up, but the fact that issues are coming up repeatedly.

Scene 12: Giving thanks

The main difficulty is expressing needs and feelings sincerely.

Notes and References

Notes

1. Names used in this book are unisex, and the gender-neutral they/their is used wherever it's possible without compromising readability (e.g., in dialogue). In other cases, a gender is either chosen randomly or, when referring to real people, the corresponding gender is used.
2. I choose to make my troll male, though, according to what I've read, the earliest legends refer to a female troll. I leave the reader to decide which troll gender they prefer to imagine.
3. This description of "assessment tyranny" is inspired by the work of Françoise Kourilsky (Kourilsky), herself building on Alain Cayrol's "language compass" and John Grinder and Richard Bandler's metamodel.
4. The Treaty of Versailles is an excellent example of how emotional reasoning and negative intentions can cause lasting damage. The victorious allies approached the treaty discussions after World War I with the express intention of making the losers pay for the cost of the war, and the results of the injustices they imposed are still felt around the world today.
5. These presuppositions come from what's sometimes known as the "Palo Alto school of psychology". The term is used to refer to an approach to psychological therapy which revolutionized therapy in the 1960s. Gregory Bateson led the movement and it is renowned for the establishment of Brief Therapy and the Systemic Approach (see "Gregory Bateson").

6. As a Verification Engineer, I used to check the implementation of integrated circuit designs before they went to the factory for manufacture. Our team motto was "Trust and Verify." We assumed that the designers had done a great job. However, in spite of that confidence, we checked!
7. Note that the preceding recommendation of starting with positive initial assumptions is also part of the systemic approach.
8. Kim Scott is the co-founder of the company Radical Candor and author of a book by the same name. She was also a CEO coach at Dropbox, Qualtrics, Twitter, and other tech companies.
9. For example, Roger Fisher and William Nury, Getting to Yes (Fisher).
10. Eric Berne, creator of the Transactional Analysis system in psychology and author of Games People Play (Berne), suggested that there are six different ways in which humans spend their time: withdrawal, rituals, pastimes, activities, games, and intimacy. I leverage this model in this book but refer to activities as "dialogue" and intimacy as "the candid exchange."
11. Not all difficult conversations involve games when considered from a strictly theoretical point of view. One-off confrontations do not have the repetitive aspect of games, for example. However, even if such a confrontation is not a game in the strict sense, Karpman's Drama Triangle is invariably useful for understanding its dynamics (Karpman). We can therefore consider it to be a game, albeit a truncated one.
12. These tendencies are well summarized in the Process Communication Model ("Process Communication Model"), which was developed from the Process Therapy Model (Kahler).
13. Prevail : prove more powerful or superior, persuade (someone) to do something (Oxford Languages)
14. Thomas d'Ansembourg Is a psychotherapist and certified trainer in NonViolent Communication. He teaches this approach, which he most often calls the Non-Violent Consciousness process (in French, "le processus de Conscience Non-Violente") and

has written several popular books - see d'Ansembourg in the Bibliography.
15. See the Communication Channel concept in The Process Communication Model ("Process Communication Model").
16. As an exercise, you might reformulate the latter request to remain assertive but leave the other party with some options.
17. Rosenberg expressed the concept of fight or flight as rebel or submit.
18. In this context, a "thing" might be a project, a technology, a document - anything that is relevant to our conversation that is not sentient.
19. The NonViolent Communication methodology (Rosenberg) distinguishes Connection Requests and Action Requests.
20. A word of caution: even these well-meaning interruptions may be ill advised when the other person is angry or irritated. When faced with someone in this state, attentive listening is usually the best way to restore calm. Almost anything I say will trigger more anger or irritation.
21. Madeleine Albright(1937–2022) was an American diplomat and political scientist who served as the 64th United States Secretary of State from 1997 to 2001. A member of the Democratic part, one of her last contributions to the world was to teach a Masterclass on Diplomacy with her counterpart Condoleeza Rice (a Republican, and also a former Secretary of State). See https://www.masterclass.com/classes/madeleine-albright-and-condoleezza-rice-teach-diplomacy.
22. The study (Guillaud) was carried out by Shai Danziger of Ben Gurion University in Neguev, Israel, and Jonathan Levav, Professor of Marketing at Columbia Business School, analyzes the results of 1,112 parole hearings from Israeli prisons over a 10-month period, conducted by 8 judges with an average of 22 years' seniority.
23. Jon Kabat-Zinn (born June 5, 1944) is an American professor emeritus of medicine and the creator of the Stress Reduction

Clinic and the Center for Mindfulness in Medicine, Health Care, and Society at the University of Massachusetts Medical School. He teaches mindfulness, with the primary aim of helping people cope with stress, anxiety, pain, and illness.
24. Rebecca Shafir is a speech and language pathologist, and communication consultant. She has written books on speaking and listening, and *The Zen of Listening* can be found in the Works Cited section.
25. I often see static points of view develop as the unfortunate result of careful planning. For example, a manager informing a team member about poor performance may think of many justifications for the ratings they have awarded and the recovery action they envisage then, challenged by the lack of reaction to their initial announcement, they just keep talking and lose their connection with their collaborator. Another common example is that of a job candidate who prepares a comprehensive summary of their background and experience. Then, when given the chance, they deliver the whole thing in one go, at the expense of good interaction with the interviewer.
26. Those familiar with NonViolent Communication (Rosenberg) may recognize some of the principles described in the following subsections. At the heart of NonViolent Communication is a four-part protocol where the first three parts concern the expression of observations, feelings, and needs. I deal with all these aspects of a candid exchange under the single heading, "Explain", since I wish to give the pause, ask, listen, and explain aspects of the exchange equal weight.
27. Needs and types of needs have also been enumerated by, for example, the NonViolent Communication community. There are many needs lists, too long to remember but interesting to consult and play with. For example: https://www.cnvc.org/training/resource/needs-inventory and https://communicationbienveillante.eu/cnvbesoin/

28. Socrates (c. 470–399 BCE) was a Greek philosopher credited as the founder of Western philosophy. He authored no texts and is known mainly through the posthumous accounts of classical writers, written as dialogues in which Socrates examines a subject in the style of question and answer. He was sentenced to death for impiety and corrupting the Athenian youth and forced to take his own life. According to one of the dialogues, his last words were a request to a friend to make good the loan of a cock that he owed a neighbor.

29. Esther Perel is a psychotherapist who studies and teaches the importance of trust, freedom, security, and eroticism in modern partnerships. According to Esther, "It is the quality of our relationships that determines the quality of our lives."

30. In programming circles, it's common practice to keep a rubber duck close at hand, not because programmers bathe more frequently than other people but because they use rubber ducks to help debug code. By explaining a bug to their duck, they force themselves to structure the issue clearly, and very often a solution occurs to them. When I make an inquiry to get the other person talking, I trigger this beneficial "rubber duck effect."

31. Sir Isaiah Berlin OM CBE FBA (1909–1997) was a Russian-British social and political theorist, philosopher, and historian of ideas. Although he became averse to writing for publication, many of his spoken words were converted into published essays and books, both by himself and by others. His lifelong opposition to violence began with his experiences of the February Revolution in Russia.

32. In The Crooked Timber of Humanity (Berlin), Isaiah Berlin wrote, "To force people into the neat uniforms demanded by dogmatically believed-in schemes is almost always the road to inhumanity. We can only do what we can: but that we must do, against difficulties. Of course, social or political collisions will take place; the mere conflict of positive values alone makes this unavoidable. Yet they can, I believe, be minimized by promoting

and preserving an uneasy equilibrium, which is constantly threatened and in constant need of repair—that alone, I repeat, is the precondition for decent societies and morally acceptable behavior; otherwise, we are bound to lose our way."
33. Commanding someone to be spontaneous is an example of a "double bind," which Myriam-Webster defines as "a psychological predicament in which a person receives from a single source conflicting messages that allow no appropriate response to be made."
34. As George Harrison (singer, songwriter and lead guitarist of The Beatles) pointed out, "We are one and life goes on within you and without you". Food for thought!
35. Lucius Annaeus Seneca the Younger (c. 4 BCE—CE 65) was a Stoic philosopher, statesman, and dramatist in Ancient Rome, and is credited with the line, "It is not because things are difficult that we do not dare; it is because we do not dare that they are difficult." He was an advisor to Nero and was forced to take his own life for participating in a conspiracy, of which he was probably innocent. His stoic and calm suicide was much admired.

Works Cited

Alcantara, P. de. (2013). *Indirect procedures: A musician's guide to the Alexander technique.* Oxford University Press.

Altucher, James. "5 Ways To Do Nothing and Become More Productive." https://www.behance.net/blog/5-ways-to-do-nothing-and-become-more-productive. May 2024.

"Behance." *Behance.net,* https://www.behance.net/blog/5-ways-to-do-nothing-and-become-more-productive. May 2024.

Berlin, Isaiah. *The Crooked Timber of Humanity.* 2nd ed., Pimlico, 2013.

Berne, Eric. *Games People Play: The Psychology of Human Relationships.* Penguin Books, 2010.

Betts, Andrew. *Client Encounters of the Technical Kind, Chapter 8, Challenging and Negotiating*.

Betts, Andrew K. *Client Encounters of the Technical Kind: How to Win, Support and Challenge Customers ... Methodically, with Icon9's Tools & Best Practices for Field Engineers*. Iconda Publishing, 2015.

de Saint-Exupery, Antoine. *Airman's Odyssey: Wind, Sand and Stars, Night Flight, and Flight to Arras*. Mariner Books, 2012.

Derks, Daantje, et al. "The Role of Emotion in Computer-Mediated Communication: A Review." *Computers in Human Behavior*, vol. 24, no. 3, 2008, pp. 766–785, doi:10.1016/j.chb.2007.04.004.

Fisher, Roger, and William Ury. *Getting to Yes: Negotiating an Agreement without Giving In*. 3rd ed., Random House Business Books, 2012.

Guillaud, Hubert. "Comment prenons-nous nos décisions?" *Le Monde*, Le Monde, 13 May 2011, https://www.lemonde.fr/week-end/article/2011/05/13/comment-prenons-nous-nos-decisions_1521812_1477893.html.

Kahneman, Daniel. *Thinking, Fast and Slow*. Macat Library, 2018.

Kabat-Zinn, Jon. *Wherever You Go, There You Are: Mindfulness Meditation in Everyday Life*. Hachette Go.

Kahler, Taibi. *The Process Therapy Model: The Six Personality Types with Adaptations*. Taibi Kahler Associates, Inc., 2008.

Karpman, Stephen B. *A Game Free Life: The Definitive Book on the Drama Triangle and the Compassion Triangle by the Originator and Author. Drama Triangle Productions*. 2014.

Kourilsky, Françoise. "Du Désir Au Plaisir De Changer - 5e Éd." *Coaching et Management Du Changement*. Dunod, 2022 (French).

Lenhardt, Vincent. Outil 2: La Troisième Écoute. Youtube, 19 Aug. 2021, https://www.youtube.com/watch?v=E65Rxo6qcrI (French).

Levine, Emma E., et al. "Difficult Conversations: Navigating the Tension between Honesty and Benevolence." *Current Opinion in Psychology*, vol. 31, 2020, pp. 38–43, doi:10.1016/j.copsyc.2019.07.034.

Nutshell, Kurzgesagt –. In. *The Internet Is Worse than Ever – Now What?* Youtube, 29 Nov. 2023, https://www.youtube.com/watch?v=fuFlMtZmvY0.

Perel, Esther. "Relational Intelligence." *Masterclass.com*, https://www.masterclass.com/classes/esther-perel-teaches-relational-intelligence. May 2024.

Perel, Esther. "What Couples Therapy Can Teach Us about Conflict in the Workplace." Estherperel.com, https://www.estherperel.com/blog/conflict-in-the-workplace. May 2024.

Process Communication Model. Dec. 2021, *https://processcommunicationmodel.com*.

"Racket Feeling." *Behavenet.com*, https://www.behavenet.com/racket-feeling. May 2024.

Rahman, Toni. *Self Abuse & the Inner Drama Triangle Workbook: Transforming the IDT & Learning to Parent Yourself Well*. Independently Published, 2019.

Rimé, Bernard, et al. "Intrapersonal, Interpersonal, and Social Outcomes of the Social Sharing of Emotion." *Current Opinion in Psychology*, vol. 31, 2020, pp. 127–134, doi:10.1016/j.copsyc.2019.08.024.

Rosenberg, Marshall B. *Nonviolent Communication: A Language of Life: Create Your Life, Your Relationships, and Your World in Harmony with Your Values*. PuddleDancer Press, 2007.

Seligman, Martin. *Authentic Happiness: Using the New Positive Psychology to Realise Your Potential for Lasting Fulfilment*. Hachette UK, 2011.

Schutz, Will. *The Human Element: Productivity, Self-Esteem and the Bottom Line*. Jossey-Bass, 1994.

Scott, Kim. *Radical Candor: Be a Kick-Ass Boss without Losing Your Humanity*. St Martin's Press, 2019.

Shafir, Rebecca Z. "The Zen of Listening: Mindful Communication in the Age of Distraction." *Quest Books*, 2012.

Shakespeare, William. "The Tragedy of Hamlet, Prince of Denmark." *The Oxford Shakespeare: Hamlet*, edited by George Richard Hibbard, Oxford University Press, 1603, pp. 138–140.

Suzuki, Shunryu. *Beginner's Mind: 50th Anniversary Edition*. Shambhala Publications, 2020.

"Maslow's Hierarchy of Needs." *Wikipedia, The Free Encyclopedia*, May 2024, https://en.wikipedia.org/w/index.php?title=Maslow%27s_hierarchy_of_needs&oldid=1225111638.

"Gregory Bateson." *Wikipedia, The Free Encyclopedia*, May 2024, https://en.wikipedia.org/w/index.php?title=Gregory_Bateson&oldid=1224236469.

"Mind Map." *Wikipedia, The Free Encyclopedia*, Mar. 2024, https://en.wikipedia.org/w/index.php?title=Mind_map&oldid=1214957919.

"PechaKucha." *Wikipedia, The Free Encyclopedia*, Mar. 2024, https://en.wikipedia.org/w/index.php?title=PechaKucha&oldid=1214973614.

"Sketchnoting." *Wikipedia, The Free Encyclopedia*, Aug. 2023, https://en.wikipedia.org/w/index.php?title=Sketchnoting&oldid=1172106005.

"Suspension of Disbelief." *Wikipedia, The Free Encyclopedia*, May 2024, https://en.wikipedia.org/wiki/Suspension_of_disbelief.

Bibliography

Berlin, Isaiah. *The Crooked Timber of Humanity*. 2nd ed., Pimlico, 2013.

Berne, Eric. *Games People Play: The Psychology of Human Relationships*. Penguin Books, 2010.

Betts, Andrew K. *Client Encounters of the Technical Kind: How to Win, Support and Challenge Customers*. Iconda Publishing, 2015.

d'Ansembourg, Thomas. *Cessez d'Être Gentil, Soyez Vrai!: Être Avec Les Autres En Restant Soi-Même*. Édition Du Club Québec Loisirs, 2001 (French).

d'Ansembourg, Thomas, *Être Heureux, Ce N'est Pas Nécessairement Confortable*. [Montréal] : Édition du Club Québec loisirs, 2004 (French).

Fisher, Roger, and William Ury. *Getting to Yes: Negotiating an Agreement without Giving In*. 3rd ed., Random House Business Books, 2012.

Jung, Carl. *Modern Man in Search of a Soul*. Lushena Books, 2023.

Kahneman, Daniel. *Thinking, Fast and Slow*. Macat Library, 2018.

Patterson, Kerry, et al. *Crucial Conversations: Tools for Talking When Stakes Are High*. McGraw-Hill Contemporary, 2002.

Perel, Esther. "Relational Intelligence." *Masterclass.com*, https://www.masterclass.com/classes/esther-perel-teaches-relational-intelligence. May 2024.

Rahman, Toni. *Self Abuse & the Inner Drama Triangle Workbook: Transforming the IDT & Learning to Parent Yourself Well*. Independently Published, 2019.

Rosenberg, Marshall B. *Nonviolent Communication: A Language of Life: Create Your Life, Your Relationships, and Your World in Harmony with Your Values*. PuddleDancer Press, 2007.

Showkeir, Jamie, and Maren Showkeir. *Authentic Conversations: Moving from Manipulation to Truth and Commitment: Moving from Manipulation to Truth and Commitment*. Berrett-Koehler, 2008.

■

Andrew Keith Betts PhD is an independent consultant to the Electronic Design Automation Industry and a member of the European Mentoring and Coaching Council —an accredited Senior Practitioner. Also an experienced trainer, he regularly gives courses on professional communication to companies in Europe, the USA, and Asia.

Andy is based in Crolles, near Grenoble in France, and has dual French and British nationality. He runs his professional activities through his company, ICONDA Solutions. For recommendations of his work and other information and contact details, please see:

https://www.linkedin.com/in/andrewkbetts/
https://iconda.solutions/

www.ingramcontent.com/pod-product-compliance
Ingram Content Group UK Ltd.
Pitfield, Milton Keynes, MK11 3LW, UK
UKHW020245240426
12048UKWH00026B/1628